Mastering the BizTalk Technical Interview

200 BizTalkTechnical Questions with Answers

Moustafa Refaat

To my dear brother,
Thank you

Table of Contents

About the Author

Moustafa is the founder of Genetic Thought Software, A software company committed to delivering superior software and consulting services. Moustafa have been intensely involved with BizTalk products since 2004. Moustafa has developed, designed and architectured many systems with the BizTalk product family including BizTalk 2002, 2004, 2006 and 2006 R2. Moustafa has more than 20 years of experience developing software solutions, leading the Architecture, Design, and Refactoring of many large projects. At LV Intl Moustafa provided Architecture Guidance and BizTalk Knowledge transfer to guide the upgrade of the client integration applications to BizTalk 2006. At Deloitte DMGF, Moustafa salvaged the ADP project, provided technical guidance to establish self reliant BizTalk group. At Newfoundland and Labrador Prescription Drug Plan Project, Moustafa delivered a superior solution to integrating feeds from pharmacies, government, drug price providers and adjunction software. At FCT, Moustafa have led the architecture for several project in parallel, Motion (Releases 7, 8 and 9), Integrating with 3rd party providers (PPSA/Chattel Project) and the identity management initiative among others. Moustafa holds IEEE/CSDP, MCSD (6.0, and .Net) and Oracle certifications. Moustafa acted as a referee for the IEEE Software magazine.

Moustafa can be reached at Moustafa@MoustafaRefaat.com or you can read his blog at http://www.MoustafaRefaat.com

Introduction

General

Not being prepared is preparing to Failure! Ironic but true. Interviewing is just like any other skill that you have acquired; the more that you practice it the better you will get at it. The art of interviewing is as important as other skills that you bring to the table as an IT specialist. The job market is a competitive place and in many cases the only difference between whether you get an offer or not will come down to the way you handle yourself in the interview. What follows is a summary of tips that I have compiled after observing the habits of the most successful people in the business.

You are being interviewed because they selected you out of a large pool of potential candidates. This should act as a boost to your confidence because in a way you have already started on the right foot with the interviewer. Think of the interview as a chance to prove to them that they are right about you!

Take care of the basics in advance and remove the obstacles ahead of time. Often the outcome of an interview is the opposite of what you expected. There have been several situations when a consultant least likely to be hired gets the contract. Conversely, a person seen as being the "perfect" fit for a job does not get the assignment. The only variable that consistently explains such outcomes is the amount of time and effort a person puts into preparing for the interview. Thorough preparation is often what stands between you and your next assignment.

Your goal is to generate an offer in all cases. Remember that you can always say no to an offer that you do get but you can never say yes to one that you do not get. It is not uncommon for people to lose their enthusiasm during an interview if they find out something about the job that seems unappealing to them. If this happens to you it is important to keep in mind that things are not always what they appear to be.

The hiring manager needs to know three things:

1. Are you a team player, good person, will they get along with you?
2. Are you capable of doing the work?
3. Do you want the position? (The best results are when the interviewee conveys 80% enthusiasm and 20% technology knowledge in the interview)

All that you have to do is convince them that the answer to all three questions is YES.

Proving that you are capable

When an interviewer is asking technical questions about your experience in a particular area, THIS IS NOT THE TIME TO BE HUMBLE! Always answer their questions with an example of where and how you used that skill before. Avoid yes or no answers;

develop answers to match the needs of the customer's project. To sell your skills effectively, you can follow a simple three step format

1. Simply outline what you are selling.
2. Qualify or explain what you are selling.
3. Finally, relate what you are selling to the customer's need.

Show them that you want it

It is important to come across as "in to it" as possible. All things considered equal the person that appears to want the job the most will get the offer. Try to find out if their level of interest in you by asking them directly. Good questions to ask are:

1. Do you feel that I am suitable for the position?
2. Do you have any reservations about my ability to do this job?

Don't be afraid to ask these questions, you may be able to overcome any objections that they may have. It may feel a bit uncomfortable but it is better to find out what their concerns are than it is to find out that you did not get the job. Asking for the job can be a crucial factor in the interviewer's decision-making process.

Practice, Practice, Practice

Preparing for interviews is critical to the success of IT Contract Consultant. Treat every interview as the most important marketing presentation that your business will make. You have one opportunity to convince a customer of your abilities. Make every phrase, word and gesture count. This may all seem like common sense to you, but practicing in front of a mirror or with a partner will make you more at ease and add to your successful at interviewing. All professionals practice their sport to stay sharp. Finally, as Yoda says, do not try, just do it!

The Questions

I have collected the following 200 questions through interviews I have conducted and interviews that I was the applicant. I also collected them from the online user groups and other websites. I have prepared the answers and reviewed them as best as I can. If you happen to fall on a question that I did not include here or you want to discuss any of the answers that I have provided please email me at Moustafa@MoustafaRefaat.com.

Moustafa Refaat

Toronto, April 2008

Basic Questions

1. What is BizTalk?

BizTalk Server is a Business Process Management and Service Oriented Architecture or Enterprise Services Bus SOA/ESB platform. You can think of BizTalk Server as a group of application services that facilitate the rapid creation of integration solutions. BizTalk Server is designed specifically to integrate disparate systems in a loosely coupled way. BizTalk Server is a toolkit, and within this toolkit you will find tools to help you build your application. Combining different systems into effective business processes is a challenging problem. The heart of BizTalk is the BizTalk Server Engine. The engine has two main parts:

- A messaging component that provides the ability to communicate with a range of other software. By relying on adapters for different kinds of communication, the engine can support a variety of protocols and data formats, including Web services and many others.
- Support for creating and running graphically-defined processes called orchestrations. Built on top of the engine's messaging components, orchestrations implement the logic that drives all or part of a business process.

Several other components can also be used in concert with the engine, including:

- A Business Rule Engine that evaluates complex sets of rules.
- A Health and Activity Tracking tool that lets developers and administrators monitor and manage the engine and the orchestrations it runs.
- An Enterprise Single Sign-On (SSO) facility that provides the ability to map authentication information between Windows and non-Windows systems.

On top of this foundation, BizTalk Server includes a group of technologies that address the more business-oriented needs of information workers. Those technologies are:

- Business Activity Monitoring, which information workers can use to monitor a running business process. The information is displayed in business rather than technical terms, and business users determine what information is displayed.
- Business Activity Services, which information workers can use to set up and manage interactions with transacting partners.

2. What Is a BizTalk Application?

A BizTalk application is a logical grouping of the items, called "artifacts," used in a BizTalk Server business solution. Artifacts include the following:

- BizTalk assemblies and the BizTalk-specific resources that they contain – orchestrations, pipelines, schemas, and maps
- .NET assemblies that do not contain BizTalk-specific resources
- Policies
- Send ports, send port groups, receive locations, and receive ports
- Other items that are used by the solution, such as certificates, COM components, and scripts

3. What is a pipeline?

A pipeline is a component of Microsoft BizTalk Server that provides an implementation of the Pipes and Filters integration pattern. During the receiving and sending of messages, a pipeline performs transformations on messages to prepare them to enter or leave BizTalk Server **MessageBox**. The main Task of a pipeline is to convert input data into proper XML.

4. What are the types of pipelines?

There are two types of pipelines, send pipelines and receive pipelines, and these match the ports (Send Ports and Receive ports) in which they execute. Send pipelines are executed in send ports and in the response portion of a request/response receive port, while receive pipelines are executed in receive locations, and in the response portion of a solicit/response send port. Essentially, receive pipelines are intended to be used to transform messages that are being published to the **MessageBox** database, while send pipelines are intended to be used on messages which are being sent out of BizTalk Server.

5. What is BPEL?

BPEL is a standard for specification of business processes; BPEL is targeted at business process interop rather than cross-platform execution. BPEL is an Orchestration language. An orchestration specifies an executable process that involves message exchanges with other systems, such that the message exchange sequences are controlled by the orchestration designer.

6. What are the out of the box pipelines?

There are four out of the box pipelines (also referred to as default pipelines) :

- **PassThruReceive pipeline:** The pass-through receive pipeline has no components. It is used for simple pass-through scenarios when no message payload processing is necessary. This pipeline is generally used when the source and the destination of the message are known, and the message requires no validation, encoding, or disassembling. This pipeline is commonly used in conjunction with the pass-through send pipeline. Because it does not contain a disassembler, the pass-through receive pipeline cannot be used to route messages to orchestrations. The pass-through receive pipeline does not support property promotion.

- **PassThruTransmit pipeline:** The pass-through-send pipeline has no components. This pipeline is generally used when no document processing is necessary before sending the message to a destination.

- **XMLReceive pipeline:** The XML receive pipeline consists of the following stages:
  - Decode. Empty
  - Disassemble. Contains the XML Disassembler component
  - Validate. Empty
  - ResolveParty. Runs the Party Resolution component, which resolves the certificate subject or the source security ID to the party ID.

- **XMLSend pipeline:** The XML send pipeline consists of the following stages:
  - Pre-assemble. Empty
  - Assemble. Contains the XML Assembler component
  - Encode. Empty

7. What is the lifecycle of a Message in BizTalk server?

A message is received through a receive location defined in a given receive port. This message is processed by the pipeline associated with the receive location, and if there are any inbound maps associated with the receive port they are executed. The resulting message is then published to the **MessageBox** database. The **MessageBox** evaluates active subscriptions and routes the message to those orchestrations, and send ports with matching subscriptions. Orchestrations may process the message and publish messages through the **MessageBox** to a send port where it is pushed out to its final destination.

8. What is Routing with the Message Type?

One of the message properties is the message type. To use message type in routing, it must be promoted into the context.

9. What is the Hub and Spoke Model?

A hub, is (a software application, or server) that accepts requests from multiple applications (the spokes). Applications interact with the hub through adapters (or interfaces) deployed on the hub, and as such, hub and spoke do not require any modifications to the existing applications and support a wide variety of transports.

10. What is the Message Bus Model?

The Message bus consists of a network of message processing functionality interlinked through a common bus-specific protocol.

11. What is the Publish and Subscribe Architecture of BizTalk?

The publish/subscribe architecture consists of three components:

- Publishers: like receive ports that publish messages that arrive in their receive locations, orchestrations that publish messages when sending messages or starting another orchestration asynchronously, and solicit/response send ports that publish messages when they receive a response from the target application or transport.

- Subscribers: like send ports, or orchestrations.

- Events: are signals that indicate the arrival of a new message or changes to the subscriptions.

12. What is a Message?

A message is a finite entity within the BizTalk **MessageBox**. Messages have context properties and zero-to-many message parts. Subscriptions match particular context properties for a message and determine endpoints, which are interested in processing it. Messages are immutable once they are published to the **MessageBox**. Messages are comprised of zero or more message parts. All messages with parts generally have a part that is marked as the body part. The body part of the message is considered to contain the data or "meat" of the message.

13. What is an interchange?

An Interchange is a message, or a series of messages, that flows through the **MessageBox**. Generally one message is equivalent (or equal to) to one Interchange. The Interchange is uniquely identified by the **InterchangeID** promoted property. In many cases, the Interchange contains more than one message. This is often the case when processing flat-file documents or XML documents that contain envelopes. In this case, there will be one Interchange with as many messages as were contained in the original envelope. Each message would have the same InterchangeID. However, they would all have unique **MessageID**. In pipeline development, only Disassembler and Assembler components need to be concerned about this, since all other components receive one message and return one message. Disassemblers will receive one message and de-batch it into many messages, and the reverse is the case with Assemblers.

14. What is an orchestration?

An Orchestration is an executable business process that can subscribe to (receive) and publish (send) messages through the MessageBox database. In addition, an orchestration can construct new messages.

15. What is the Rules Engine?

The **Business Rule Engine** (BRE) is an effective way to define a business process as set of rules. These rules can be created and modified by business-oriented users using a tool called the Business Rule Composer. Using the BRE, developers can quickly and easily change rules as needed.

To appreciate the value of these tools, think about what is required to change a business rule that has been implemented within an orchestration. A developer must first open the orchestration in Visual Studio 2005, modify the appropriate shapes (and perhaps the .NET or COM objects they invoke), and then build and deploy the modified assembly. Doing this also requires stopping and restarting the BizTalk application that includes this orchestration. If instead, this business rule is implemented using BRE, it can be modified without recompiling or restarting anything. All what's needed is to use the Business Rule Composer to change the desired rule, and then, redeploy the new set of rules. The change takes effect immediately. And while orchestrations are typically created and maintained by developers, business rules are readable enough that in some cases they can be modified by business analysts without the need to involve more technical people.

General Questions

16. What are the different BizTalk editions when would you use each one?

There are four different Editions of BizTalk:

- Enterprise
- Standard
- Branch
- Developer

You would normally use the developer edition for the development environment; use the standard if you have a small solution that does not need failover and recovery. I have used the standard edition mostly for solutions that are mainly batch processing (for example, pushing the sales data to the accounting system at the end of the day); it is suitable for when the business can live with the fact that the system might not be available for a short time due to IT maintenance, failures, etc. On all other implementations, especially in the case of online processing, you will have to go with the Enterprise. The Applications number should not be the determining factor in your decision. Creating too many applications comes with it nuisances, so be careful when designing a large number of applications for a solution.

17. Does BizTalk support synchronous communication?

BizTalk Server architecture is asynchronous for scalability reasons. However, the architecture of the BizTalk Messaging Engine enables exposing a synchronous message exchange pattern on top of these asynchronous exchanges. To do this, the engine handles the complex task of correlating the request and response messages across a scaled-out architecture by linking together a number of asynchronous message exchanges to expose a synchronous interface.

18. What is the Optimal BizTalk project architecture or design? How would you structure your code?

There is no such thing as "Optimal BizTalk Project Architecture". Though there is the most suitable architecture and design for each solution. There are many questions you need to consider when designing a solution.

1. The organization environment? Organization IT standards how are they going to affect the solution you will deliver?

2. The project requirements? Business requirements, software requirements?

3. The staff that will be working with you on the project, or would be supporting the solution after solution delivery.

4. How would you layer your project? Are you going to use the famous interface, logic, data access layers or you are going to use more. One example of more than one layer is shown in the following example in Figure 1.

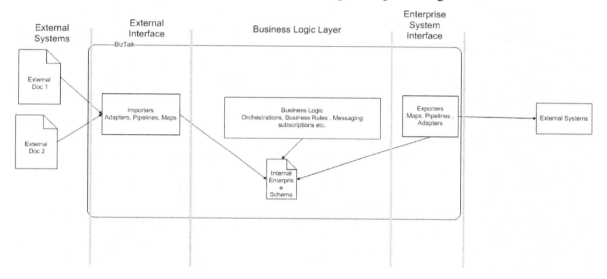

Figure 1: General BizTalk Based Solution

As Figure 1 shows, designing your solution in a layered manner is the best option. You can design the solution to consist of the three following layers

1. External Interface Layer: this layer contains all different maps, pipelines, schemas that would consume external data feeds and convert them to a unified internal schema that is internal to your enterprise. This can be implemented in a DLL or several DLLS, one DLL per feed, or several DLLs per feed. It depends on your solution, future changes (new third parties, external systems etc)

2. The Business Logic Layer: this is where all your business logic gets implemented in orchestrations, maps, business rule polices, etc.

3. Enterprise System Interface: This layer is similar to the External Interface layer except it is for internal systems in the enterprise.

You should note that we are always changing to unified or a simple schema internal to the system. I have seen many BizTalk solutions where they had so many orchestrations,

AICs, which are performing the same logic only because the third party supplied schemas were different.

On any BizTalk solution you should strive to

1. Maximize the use of the BizTalk out-of-box features, and utilities.

2. Minimize the amount of code (this includes, custom pipeline components, custom adapters, custom libraries, etc). Yes, we developers love to write code, but you have to remember that the purpose is to deliver a robust, reliable, and cost effective solution to the organization you are working with. From that perspective, any custom code you write is at least 10 times costlier. Why you ask, well any custom code you write, you are in a way wasting your talent by reinventing the wheel. If there is an available library, feature, or toolkit, that does what you need to do, or need small tweaking to do what you want to do, it is more cost effective to the organization as it will have industry standard robustness. And most importantly the organization does not have to maintain it (fix the bugs; upgrade the code when a new version of BizTalk becomes available).

3. Prefer to buy components that are not out of the box from BizTalk than developing them. The same argument in point 2 applies here too.

As for structuring the code, there is no single answer to fit every solution, there is a tendency by many BizTalk developers to have all the schemas in a project, all maps in a project, all orchestrations in a project, and all pipeline in a project. That is not suitable for large, medium and sometimes not even for small solutions. When you are structuring your solution code, you should consider deployment of the DLLs and other artifacts, the modularity of the solution for example adding new partners, functionality should be easy. You should also consider minimizing the dependency between developers, if all developers working on the same project, they can hinder each other's progress, also if one developer is specialized in schemas, then other developers are dependent on her and waiting for her to finish the code so they can start.

---

19. What is a host group? Which host group does a user need to belong to in order to submit messages to the message box?

A host group is the Windows group (the default is named "BizTalk Application Users"). You use for accounts with access to the in-process BizTalk host. You can only associate a host with one Windows group (called a host group). The host group must have a SQL Server login and privileges to all relevant BizTalk Server databases. When you associate a host with the host group, you grant the host the privileges of that host group.

The host group requires the following privileges:

- It must be a member of the BTS_HOST_USERS SQL Server role in the following databases:

- BizTalk Management (known as the Configuration database in BizTalk Server 2004)
- MessageBox
- Rule Engine
- Tracking
- BAM Primary Import

- It must be a member of the BTS_<in-process host name>_USERS SQL Server role for the MessageBox database
- It must also be a member of the BAM_EVENT_WRITER SQL Server role in the BAM Primary Import database.

20. What is content-based routing?

"Content-based routing" is routing messages based on envelope properties, or simply based on receive port configuration properties. The dynamic routing of content is implemented by creating filters for specified properties on send ports and send port groups. Note that dynamic routing is based on properties of the document, not necessarily the content of the document. Routing can be performed based on information contained in the envelope of the document or even configuration information from the receive location.

21. How many Servers are required to implement a BizTalk Solution?

From the logical servers perspective you need at least a MS SQL Server, and a BizTalk Server. If you are going to use Web Services based on ASP.Net, then you will also need an IIS Server. As for the number of physical servers, this would depend on the load and the expected performance that the system would support.

22. What is a BizTalk Host?

A BizTalk host is nothing more than a logical container. Hosts provide the ability to structure the processing of your application into groups that can be distributed across multiple memory processes and across machines. A host is most often used to separate adapters, orchestrations, and ports to run on separate machines to aid in load balancing.

23. What is a Host Instance?

A host instance is just that, an instance of the host. The instance is actually just a service that runs on the machine called BTSNTSvc.exe. This process provides the BizTalk engine a place to execute, and allows for instances of different hosts to be running on one machine at a given time. Each host will end up being a separate instance of the BTSNTSvc.exe service from within the Windows Task Manager.

24. What is the difference between an Isolated Host and In-Process Host?

The difference is that an Isolated Host must run under another process, in most cases IIS, while an In-Process Host is a complete BizTalk service alone. Additionally, since Isolated Hosts exist outside of the BizTalk environment, the BizTalk Administration Tools are not able to determine the status of these hosts (stopped, started, or starting).

25. Can you explain the Security differences between Isolated and In Process hosts?

In-Process Hosts must run under an account that is within the In-Process host's Windows group, and do not maintain security context within the MessageBox. Isolated Hosts are useful when a service already exists that will be receiving messages either by some proprietary means, or by some other transport protocol such as HTTP. In this case, the Isolated Host only runs one instance of the End Point Manager (EPM), and is responsible for receiving messages from its transport protocol and sending them to the MessageBox through the EPM.

26. What is a BizTalk Application in BizTalk 2006?

BizTalk Applications allow an administrator to logically group artifacts according to the application that uses them. This concept is extended to the improved deployment model within BizTalk 2006, which allows the exporting of a BizTalk application to a Windows Installer package. Applications can contain any number of BizTalk artifacts such as schemas, business rules, orchestrations, and ports. To facilitate such organization, the BizTalk Management tools have been redesigned in BizTalk 2006.

27. What certificate stores does BizTalk use?

BizTalk Server relies heavily on the security provided by certificates. By using certificates for encryption and digital signatures, BizTalk Server can send and receive data that can be trusted, and can help ensure that the data it processes is secure. For both encryption and digital signatures, there is a public key certificate and a private key certificate. For encryption, the sender of the message uses the receiver's public key certificate to encrypt the message, while the receiver of the message uses its private key to decrypt the message. For digital signatures, the sender of the message uses a private key certificate to sign the message, and the receiver of the message uses the public key certificate of the sender to verify the signature. The certificate stores are:**Other People certificate store**: Public key certificates are public and accessible by anyone with access to the computer on which they are stored. BizTalk Server retrieves from this store the public key certificates to encrypt messages and to verify the digital signatures for incoming messages. All users can read and use the certificates in this store. The following figure shows the Other People certificate store that BizTalk Server uses for public key certificates.

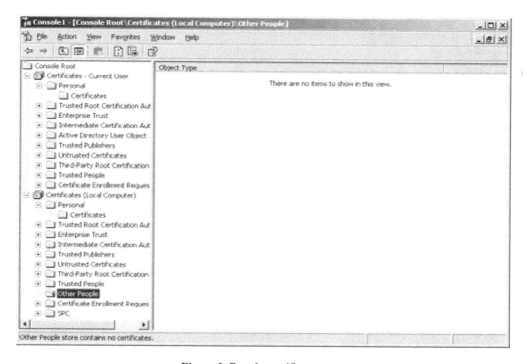

Figure 2: People certificate store

Personal certificate store: Every Windows account enabled to log on interactively on a computer has a personal certificate store that only that account can access. BizTalk Server uses the personal certificate store for the service account of each host instance to access the private key certificates to which each service account has access. The private key certificates must be stored in the Personal certificate store for the service account for each host instance on each computer that has a running host instance that requires the certificate for decryption or for signing outbound messages.

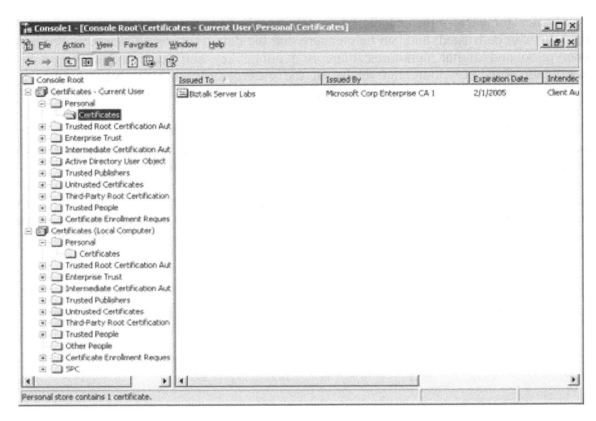

Figure 3: Personal certificate Store

For more information about the certificate stores and the Certificate snap-in for the Microsoft Management Console (MMC), search for "Certificate console" in Windows XP, Windows Server™ 2003, or Windows 2000 Server Help.

28. What is the Chain of Responsibility Pattern and how would you implement it with BizTalk?

The intent of the Chain of Responsibility pattern is to provide a loosely coupled sender/receiver relationship by providing more than one component an opportunity to handle a request. This chains all receiving components and passes the request along the chain until the request is handled.

With BizTalk, you can loosely couple the links between each concrete handler by using message queuing. This not only allows each concrete handler a loosely coupled way of receiving a request in a BizTalk-friendly manner, but it also provides a guaranteed form of delivering a request.

29. What is the Observer Pattern and how do you implement it in BizTalk?

The intent of the Observer pattern is to provide a mechanism to allow objects to subscribe dynamically to state change notifications from another object. You implement the Observer Pattern by using type publisher/subscriber-type relationship. If an observer wants to stop receiving notification, then that observer simply unsubscribe with the Observable object in similar fashion.

30. What is the Recipient List Pattern?

A content-based router allows us to route a message to the correct system based on message content. This process is transparent to the original sender in the sense that the originator simply sends the message to a channel, where the router picks it up and takes care of everything. In some cases, though, we may want to specify one or more recipients for the message. To do that, we define a channel for each recipient. Then use a Recipient List to inspect an incoming message, determine the list of desired recipients, and forward the message to all channels associated with the recipients in the list.

31. What Are Enterprise Integration Patterns?

Enterprise integration patterns provide guidance by documenting the accepted solutions to recurring problems within a given context. Patterns are abstract enough to apply to most integration technologies, but specific enough to provide hands-on guidance to designers and architects. Patterns also provide a vocabulary for developers to efficiently describe their solution.

32. Is there a special way for one message guaranteed delivery in BizTalk?

Yes, the BizTalk Framework has one approach for doing exactly-once guaranteed delivery using over-the-wire transport protocols such as HTTP or SMTP. This framework has existed since 1998, and can be thought of as a precursor to pending standards initiatives based on Web services, specifically WSReliable. Typically, the problem of guaranteed exactly-once delivery of data has been the domain of technologies like Message Queuing (also known as MSMQ). However, such technologies usually require common software at the two endpoints of a data flow, and also do nothing to address the use of open transport protocols based on public networks, such as the data that flows across enterprise boundaries by using the Internet. The BizTalk Framework implements some of the same mechanisms present in earlier attempts to solve this problem of guaranteed exactly-once delivery of data. A good example of other solutions to the problem is electronic data interchange (EDI), where ANSI X12 control numbers and standard 997 functional acknowledgment documents form the basis of guaranteeing that data is received only one time, and that the sender is notified of any problems on the receiving end. The BizTalk Framework assumes that, however disparate the systems trading data may be, they both understand the BizTalk Framework protocol requirements of:

- Using a predictable envelope format for wrapping transmissions.

- Tagging every outbound transmission with a globally unique identifier.

- Always returning to the sender an acknowledgment of receipt that includes the globally unique identifier, even for data already received, acknowledged, and processed.

- Some means by which the sender can repeat transmission until either a receipt arrives from the receiver, or some time period passes beyond which the transmission is no longer valid.

33. What is EDI Solution Architecture?

Electronic Data Interchange (EDI) usage entails message syntax and standards (including ANSI X12 and UN/EDIFACT), messaging protocol, and transports. The following are characteristics of EDI messaging:

- EDI messaging protocols ensure that data always arrives as expected, and corrupted or incorrect data is automatically detected and reported.

- EDI mechanisms usually specify data aggregation schemes (batching).

- Users often customize EDI document definitions by implementing subset or specific implementation of an EDI guideline.

- BizTalk Server processes EDI messages using receive and send pipelines specific to EDI that can parse and serialize EDI messages.

34. What is Enterprise Single Sign-On (SSO)?

SSO provides services to store and transmit encrypted user credentials across local and network boundaries, including domain boundaries. SSO stores the credentials in the SSO database. Because SSO provides a generic single sign-on solution, middleware applications and custom adapters can leverage SSO to securely store and transmit user credentials across the environment. End users do not have to remember different credentials for different applications. The Single Sign-On system consists of an SSO database, a master secret server, and one or more Single Sign-On servers.

The SSO system contains affiliate applications that an administrator defines. An affiliate application is a logical entity that represents a system or sub-system such as a host, back-end system, or line of business application to which you are connecting using Enterprise Single Sign-On. Each affiliate application has multiple user mappings; for example, it has the mappings between the credentials for a user in Active Directory and their corresponding RACF credentials.

35. What is AS2?

AS2 (Applicability Statement 2) is a way of implementing EDI over the Internet (EDIINT). The AS2 specification defines MIME-based secure peer-to-peer business data interchange. Messages containing an envelope with MIME data are transmitted using HTTP over TCP/IP. AS2 uses the HTTP POST operation to send EDI, XML, or other business data. AS2 is not restricted to sending EDI data. Request-URI identifies a process to be used to unpack and handle message data. A message disposition notification (MDN) is returned as an acknowledgment either in the HTTP response message body or by a new HTTP POST operation to a URL for the original sender.

36. Can we use Oracle instead of SQL server for the BizTalk Databases?

No, BizTalk requires the use of MS SQL Server for its databases. You can use MSDE with BizTalk Server. However, Microsoft will not support such an installation.

37. What are the BizTalk general guidelines that you should keep in mind while developing a BizTalk Solution?

- **Use the Messaging engine to the full**: if you can do some of the logic or transformations into maps and pipelines, then do not create orchestrations that do not do much but call maps.

- **Move your message transformations to the ports**: this minimizes the number of message copies created in your orchestration.

- **Avoid using XmlDoc objects in your orchestration** and use distinguished fields on a message: XmlDoc objects load the full message into a DOM and consume a considerable amount of memory resources.

- **Move data validation to the pipeline or schema**: if you are performing any data validation on your input messages, for example, validating that an order number is numeric and within a pre-specified range, you are better off specifying this form of validation when defining the data types in the schema. If you require other forms of contextual validation, you are better off doing that in a pipeline.

- **Avoid using orchestrations for routing**: if all your orchestration is doing is checking message fields to route the message to the proper handler or another worker orchestration to perform a particular task, consider redesigning that piece of your application as a set of port filters. Leverage receive ports with multiple receive locations and send groups to route messages coming in from multiple sources and send messages to multiple destinations instead of relying on orchestrations to achieve that.

- **Avoid calls to external assemblies that perform extensive processing**: especially if they call web services or make calls to a database: this holds the processing host resources and valuable host threads from servicing other orchestration instances while waiting for that external logic to terminate and return. If these calls stall or take a considerable amount of time, there is no way for the BizTalk engine to dehydrate that orchestration instance.

- **Do not wrap calls to .NET objects in atomic transactions because they are nonserializable**: if it makes sense, make this object serializable, or if it is simply a utility, use static methods instead of instantiating an object.

- **Use Parallel shapes carefully**: use parallelize receives if the order of incoming messages is unknown. The cost of persistence points associated with Parallel shapes is high.

- **Differentiate between scopes and transactions**: transaction scopes affect persistence points. Atomic transactions batch state persistence points and write them to the database in a single call. Long-running transactions, on the other hand, persists state at different points along the process. If you are not really running a transaction, do not assign a transaction type to your scope.

- **Use pass-through pipelines where possible**: the XMLSend or XMLReceive pipelines do a fair amount of work to validate and assemble the data going through them. If you are sure that outgoing and incoming messages are in a valid XML form, use a pass-through pipeline to eliminate this unneeded overhead.

- **Clean up suspended messages**: suspended messages are held in the suspended queue and thus retain an entry in the Messagebox spool table. An unexpected growth in the spool table affects overall performance, as all instances added to, changed, or removed from the system touch the spool table.

38. What are the Quality Attributes of General Software Solution?

- **Availability**: is concerned with system failure and its associated consequences. A system failure occurs when the system no longer delivers a service consistent with its specification. Such a failure is observable by the system's users. Areas of concern for availability are: how system failure is detected, how frequent it may occur, what happens when a failure occurs, how long a system is allowed to be out of operation, when failures may occur safely, how failure can be prevented, and what kinds of notifications are required when a failure occurs.
- **Modifiability**: is about the cost of change. What can be changed (the artifact)? When is the change made? And who makes the change?
- **Performance**: is about timing, Events (interrupts, messages, request from users) occur, and the system must respond to them.
- **Security**: is a measure of the system's ability to resist unauthorized usage while still providing it services to legitimate users.
- **Testability**: refers to the ease with which software can be made to demonstrate its faults testing. At least 40% of the cost of developing well engineered systems is taken up by testing.
- **Usability**: is concerned with how easy it is for the user to accomplish a desired task and the kind of user support the system provides. It can be broken into:
  - **Learning system features.**
  - **Using a system efficiently.**
  - **Minimizing the impact of errors.**
  - **Adapting the system to user needs.**
  - **Increasing confidence and satisfaction.**

Schema Design Questions

39. What is the difference between a Document Schema and a Property Schema?

A document schema is an XML schema that defines the structure of a class of XML instance messages. Because this type of schema uses XML Schema definition (XSD) language to define the structure of an XML instance message, and this is the intended purpose of XSD, such schemas use XSD in a straightforward way. Microsoft® BizTalk Server 2004 and 2006 use the XML Schema definition (XSD) language to define the structure of all messages that they process while previous versions of BizTalk used XML-Data Reduced (XDR) schemas.

A property schema is used with one of the two mechanisms that exist within BizTalk Server for what is known as property promotion. Property promotion is the process of copying specific values from deep within an instance message to the message context. From the message context, these values are more easily accessed by various BizTalk Server components. These components use the values to perform actions such as message routing. Promoted property values can also be copied in the other direction, from the more easily accessible message context back into the depths of the instance message, just before the instance message is sent to its destination. A property schema is a simple version of a BizTalk schema that plays a role in the process of copying promoted properties back and forth between the instance message and the message context.

40. How to version you Schema?

You can use the Document Version property of the Schema Node to specify the version of the schema that you are configuring. You can use whatever versioning scheme makes sense for your business. I recommend following the same versioning scheme of the assemblies i.e. 1.0.0.2 for example.

41. What is an Envelope Schema and how do you define it?

An envelope schema is a special type of XML schema. Envelope schemas are used to define the structure of XML envelopes, which are used to wrap one or more XML business documents into a single XML instance message. When you define an XML schema to be an envelope schema, a couple of additional property settings are required, depending on such factors as whether there are more than one root record defined in the envelope schema. To define a schema as an envelope schema, you need to set the Envelope property of the Schema node to the value Yes. When you define an envelope schema, you should point the envelope's Body XPath to the parent node that contains only the <any> child element. In order for the XML assembler to use the envelope, the parent node must not contain any other elements.

42. Can an envelope schema consist of more than one schema type?

Yes. XML envelopes serve two purposes within XML instance messages sent and received by Microsoft BizTalk Server:

- XML envelopes can contain data that supplements the data within the XML documents. This data can be promoted into the message context by the XML disassembler to provide easier access from a variety of BizTalk Server components. For outbound XML instance messages, the XML assembler can demote values from the message context into an envelope for inclusion in the instance message transmission.

- XML envelopes can be used to combine multiple XML documents into a single, valid XML instance message. Without an envelope to wrap multiple documents within a single root tag, an XML instance message containing multiple documents would not qualify as well-formed XML.

43. What is Flat File Schema?

A Flat File Schema defines the structure of a class of instance messages that use a flat file format, either delimited or positional or some combination thereof. Because the native semantic capabilities of XSD do not accommodate all of the requirements for defining the structure of flat file instance messages—such as the various types of delimiters that might be used for different records and fields within the flat file—BizTalk Server uses the annotation capabilities of XSD to store this extra information within an XSD schema. BizTalk Server defines a rich set of specific annotation tags that can be used to store all of the required additional information.

44. What is the difference between a Distinguished Field and a Promoted Property?

Distinguished fields are message context properties that do not require a separate property schema and that are only accessible from Orchestrations. Distinguished Fields cannot be used for routing or tracking. Since Distinguished Fields do not require a separate property schema, the evaluation of Distinguished Fields by the Orchestration engine consumes less overhead than the evaluation of Property fields by the Orchestration engine. The evaluation of Property fields requires an XPath query, while the evaluation of Distinguished Fields does not require an XPath query as the pipeline disassembler populates the Distinguished Fields in the context and the orchestration engine gets the cached values. However, if the orchestration engine does not find the property in the context, it will then evaluate the XPath query to find the value. Distinguished Fields do not have size limitations. The IsPromoted property of Distinguished Fields in the Message context is set to False.

Property Fields are message context properties that are used by the BizTalk Messaging Engine for purposes of document routing, for message tracking, and for evaluation in orchestrations. You can explicitly elevate a field in a document to the message context as a Property field by editing the schema for the document in the BizTalk Server Schema Editor that is available in Visual Studio. In order to write a field in a document to the message context as a Property Field, the document schema must have an associated property schema. Property fields are limited to 255 characters. The IsPromoted property of Property fields in the message context is set to True.

---

45. Are there any restrictions on which elements or attributes I can promote in a BizTalk Schema?

Yes Promoted properties are restricted to non-repeating elements/attributes.

---

46. How to Migrate XDR Schemas to XSD Schemas?

To generate an XSD schema from an XDR schema you use the Generated Items wizard as follows:

1. In Solution Explorer, right-click the relevant BizTalk project, point to Add, and then click Add Generated Items.

2. In the Add Generated Item - <BizTalk ProjectName> dialog box, in the Templates section, click Generate Schemas, and then click Open.

3. In the Generate Schemas dialog box, in the Document type list, select XDR Schema.

4. In the Generate Schemas dialog box, click Browse, locate the XDR schema file you want to migrate, and then click OK.

A new schema is generated from the specified XDR schema file, using the same name as that file with the .xsd extension, and then opened in BizTalk Editor

47. What is the difference between Import, Include and Redefine schema reference?

The Include reference physically includes the referenced schema definition within your schema. This allows you to access and use types defined in the included schema. You must use types in the included schema as is, or derive new types from them; no type modification is allowed. The included schema must be in the same target namespace as the including schema, or the target namespace of the included schema must be empty.

The Import allows you to accesses and use types defined in the imported schema. You must use types in the imported schema as is, or derive new types from them; no type modification allowed. However, the types can be defined in other namespaces. An imported schema must have a target namespace that is different from the importing schema.

Redefine allows you to access and use types defined in the redefined schema. You can use types in the redefined schema as is, derive new types from them, or specify modifications to them. The redefined schema must be in the same target namespace as the redefining schema, or the target namespace of the redefined schema must be empty.

---

48. How can you define an element as optional in an XSD Schema?

You can define an element to be optional by setting it's "min occurs" to 0 and it's "Max Occurs" to 1.

---

49. How can you define an element as optional in an XSD Schema?

You can define an element to be optional by setting it's "Max Occurs" to "unbounded". Note that if the BizTalk Schema editor would allow you to enter "*" but it will convert it to "unbounded".

---

50. What is the "Use Requirement" property used for?

The "Use Requirement" property is used to specify whether the selected Field Attribute node is required in an instance message. You can set it to one of the following values

- Optional: Sets the use attribute to "optional", specifying that the attribute corresponding to the selected Field Attribute node is optional in conforming instance messages.

- Prohibited: Sets the use attribute to "prohibited", specifying that the attribute corresponding to the selected Field Attribute node is not allowed in conforming instance messages. Field Attribute nodes can only be prohibited within larger structures that are being reused through derivation.

- **Required:** Sets the use attribute to "required", specifying that the attribute corresponding to the selected Field Attribute node is required in conforming instance messages. You cannot set values for the Default and Fixed properties when this property is set to **Required**.

---

51. What is the structure of a flat file?

From BizTalk Server point of view, a flat file instance message is a text file that can contain three logical parts: a header, a body, and a trailer, in that order. Both the header and the trailer are optional. For the flat file disassembler to correctly distinguish the header, the body, and the trailer of a flat file instance message, you must create and configure a separate schema for each of them. Within a particular part of a flat file instance message, different items of data are grouped into records, which themselves can contain subrecords and ultimately the individual items of data, known as fields. These records and fields are distinguished from each other using one of two different basic methods. The first method, known as positional, defines each item of data to be of a pre-established length, with pad characters being used to bring a shorter item of data up to its expected length. The second method, known as delimited, uses one or more special characters to separate items of data from each other. This method avoids the need for otherwise superfluous padding characters, but introduces some special considerations when the data itself contains the character or sequence of characters being used as a delimiter.

---

52. What are the Message Context Properties?

When a document is received by a BizTalk Server adapter, the adapter creates a BizTalk message for the document. The BizTalk message contains the document that was received as well as a message context. The message context is a container for various properties that are used by BizTalk Server when processing the document. Each property in the Message Context is composed of three parts, a name, a namespace, and a value. Message context properties are added to the message context throughout the lifetime of the message as it passes through BizTalk Server.

---

53. How to publish a Schema as a Web Service?

You use the BizTalk Web Services Publishing Wizard to create Web services that use existing schemas. You declare the Web services, Web methods, and request and response schemas that you want to publish. Using the wizard, you define the target namespace, SOAP header requirements, and the location of the generated Web service project. When you publish schemas as a Web service, you control the creation of Web services and Web methods in the BizTalk Web Services Publishing Wizard. You can rename the Web service description, Web service and Web method inside the tree available on the Web Services page. You can add and remove Web services and Web methods. The wizard uses the root element names of the selected request schemas as the input parameter name.

Pipelines and Pipeline Components Questions

54. What are the stages of a Send Pipeline?

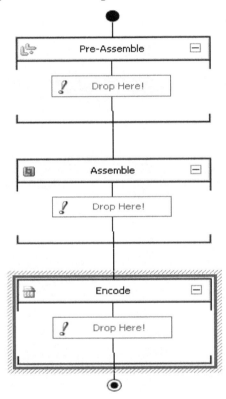

Figure 4: Send Pipeline Stages

There are three stages in a send pipeline:

- Pre-Assemble stage: where you can perform any message processing necessary before assembling the message.

- Assemble stage: where you assemble the message and prepare it to be transmitted by taking steps such as adding envelopes, converting XML to flat files, or other tasks complementary to the disassemble stage in a receive pipeline.

- Encode Stage: where you can encode or encrypt the message before delivery.

55. What are the stages of a receive pipeline?

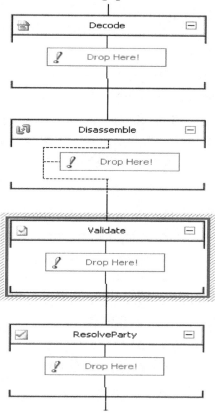

Figure 5: Receive Pipeline Stages

The receive pipeline has four stages as follows:

- Decode Stage: where you perform operations that are required to read the incoming message, for example, you will decrypt, decompress, decode, etc.

- Disassemble stage: where you disassemble an interchange into smaller messages and parse message contents. Disassemblers are used to de-batch an incoming large message into smaller ones. Each message produced by the disassemble stage is passed to the remaining stages in the pipeline.

- Validate stage: where you validate the message data, generally against a schema. Custom validate components sometime perform some kind of business validation.

- Resolve Part Stage: where you identify the BizTalk Server party associated with some security token in the message or message context.

56. What are the execution modes in a pipeline Stage?

A stage in a pipeline has an execution mode of either "All" or "First Match", which controls the components that get executed if more than one component is added to a stage.

- For stages with a mode of "All", each component is called to process the message in the order in which they are configured in the stage.

- For stages with a mode of "First Match", each component is polled to indicate that it is the right component until a match is found, at which point the component that matches is executed, while the remaining components do not get executed.

57. Which Stages has a "First Match" execution mode?

The disassemble component is the only component with a "First Match" execution mode.

58. What are the pipeline components that come out of the box in BizTalk?

The out of box or standard pipeline components are:

1. BizTalk Framework Assembler Pipeline Component.
2. BizTalk Framework Disassembler Pipeline Component.
3. Flat File Assembler Pipeline Component.
4. Flat File Disassembler Pipeline Component.
5. XML Assembler Pipeline Component.
6. XML Disassembler Pipeline Component.
7. MIME/SMIME Decoder Pipeline Component.
8. MIME/SMIME Encoder Pipeline Component.
9. Party Resolution Pipeline Component.
10. XML Validator Pipeline Component.

59. What is the BizTalk Framework Assembler Component?

The BizTalk Framework Assembler pipeline component is responsible for serializing the BizTalk Framework envelope and contents onto the message before transmission and resending in the event that a receipt does not arrive in the allotted time period. It is also responsible for receiving and processing the receipts and deleting the message instance. (A copy of the message instance of the sent message is kept in the MessageBox database until BizTalk receives a confirmation receipt from the destination. After the confirmation receipt is received, the message instance is deleted by the Messaging Engine.).

60. What is the BizTalk Framework Disassembler Pipeline Component?

The BizTalk Framework Disassembler pipeline component parses XML data and determines whether it contains a BizTalk Framework-based messaging payload. The pipeline component saves the message context, and a new message context is created with the BizTalk Framework property that needs to be generated. This property is used to route the message to the BizTalk Framework inbound handler, so it can receive the message to process. The BizTalk Framework Disassembler pipeline component generates an acknowledgment for the generated message if the sender requested one using the deliverReceiptRequest header within the BizTalk Framework envelope. This is controlled by the generate delivery receipt property in the BizTalk Framework Assembler pipeline component.

61. What is the Flat File Assembler Pipeline Component?

A Flat File Assembler combines individual documents into a batch and optionally adds a header or trailer (or both) to it. The Flat File Assembler pipeline component only supports conversions supported by the Microsoft .NET Framework. Any additional conversion can be done by writing to a custom text writer.

62. What is the Flat File Disassembler Pipeline Component?

The Flat File Disassembler component parses delimited and positional flat file format messages and converts them into an XML representation. The Flat File Disassembler also removes the header and trailer structures from the flat file message, and breaks the interchange within the message into individual documents. It also promotes properties from the documents and headers. By default, the Flat File Disassembler component does not validate documents it processes. However, you can turn validation on by setting the Validate document structure property on the component to True, or by setting the FFDasm.ValidateDocumentStructure message context property to True. The Flat File Disassembler can remove empty fields and records when suppress_empty_nodes="True" is specified by the schemaInfo annotation in the flat file XSD schema.

63. What is the XML Assembler Pipeline Component?

The XML Assembler pipeline component transfers properties from the message context back into envelopes and documents. The following actions occur in the XML Assembler component after receiving a batch of messages to form an interchange:

- The assembler creates the envelope by using the specified envelope specification.

- The component puts the content properties on the message instances by using the predefined XPaths coded as annotations in the XSD schemas associated with the message.

- The component appends the message to the envelope.

- The component puts the content properties on the envelope by using the predefined XPaths coded as annotations in the XSD schemas associated with envelopes.

64. What is the XML Disassembler pipeline component?

The XML Disassembler pipeline disassembles the received XML message as follows:

- Removing envelopes: The disassembler parses the envelope by using the envelope schemas statically associated with the component at design time, or dynamically by determining envelope schemas from the message type at run time. The schema is used to verify the structure of the envelope during envelope parsing. If envelope structure is not defined, it is found recursively by using the root node's namespace and base name to look up the schemas.

- Disassembling the interchange: The disassembler component parses each document within the envelope. For each document, the BizTalk message object is created with its own context where all the properties promoted from the envelope and from the document itself get copied. The component pulls the content properties from the envelope and message instances by using the predefined XPaths coded as annotations in the XSD schemas associated with the envelope and message. The envelope schemas as well as the individual document schemas are associated with the disassembler component in Pipeline Designer

- Promoting the content properties from interchange and individual document levels on to the message context. The XML Disassembler only processes data in the body part of the message. Thus, only properties from body part can be promoted. Datetime values from the fields associated with the promotable properties get converted to UTC when property promotion occurs. Non-body parts are copied to the output message unchanged.

65. Can you talk about the MIME/SMIME Decoder Pipeline Component?

The MIME/SMIME Decoder component provides MIME decoding functionality for messages. This pipeline component can be placed into the Decode stage of a receive pipeline. It supports 7bit, 8bit, binary, quoted-printable, UUEncode, and base64 decoding. The MIME/SMIME Decoder component can decrypt and sign-validate an incoming message. Decryption certificates are used from the personal certificate store of the current user under which the service is running. Sign-validation certificates are used from the Address Book store of the local computer or from the message itself. The MIME/SMIME Decoder pipeline component is the only out-of-the-box receive pipeline component that handles multi-part messages, including multi-part MIME/SMIME messages. The pipeline component parses the message and creates an equivalent multi-part BizTalk message. A multi-part BizTalk message has one unique part named the body part.

66. Can you discuss the MIME/SMIME Encoder Pipeline Component?

The MIME/SMIME Encoder component can be placed into the Encode stage of a send pipeline. It supports 7bit, 8bit, binary, quoted-printable, base64, and UUencode encoding. Localized data character set changes do not affect the encoding. This component can be used to either MIME encode, sign or encrypt an outgoing message with encryption and signing certificates.

67. What is the Party Resolution Pipeline Component?

The responsibility of the Party Resolution pipeline component is to map the sender certificate or the sender security identifier (SID) to the corresponding configured BizTalk Server party. When the Party Resolution component reads the incoming message, it takes two message context properties as input: WindowsUser and SignatureCertificate. The WindowsUser property is populated by the adapter, or by a custom pipeline component, with the user name of the sender when it can reliably derive the sender information. The SignatureCertificate is populated by the adapter or the MIME/SMIME Decoder pipeline component with the thumbprint of the client authentication certificate. If the message is signed, the thumbprint of the certificate that was used to validate the signature on the inbound message is then used to look in the Configuration Repository to determine which party it is associated with. If a party is found, the SourcePartyID for that party is placed in the context of the message as the originator of the message. To enable the Party Resolution pipeline component to validate a Windows user, you must add the "WindowsUser" alias to a party. If the message arrives at the Party Resolution component with both of the properties stamped, the Party Resolution component first tries to resolve the party by the certificate (assuming the Resolve Party By Certificate property is set to True). If the party is resolved, the SourcePartyID for that party is placed in the context of the message as the OriginatorPID of the message if the host process running the pipeline is marked as Authentication Trusted by the pipeline. If the party resolution cannot be completed by using the certificate, the OriginatorPID value on the message is stamped with "s-1-5-7", which is the SID of an anonymous user.

68. What is the XML Validator Pipeline Component?

The XML Validator pipeline component can be used in both send and receive pipelines in any stage except for Disassemble or Assemble. The XML Validator component validates the message against the specified schema or schemas, and if the message does not conform to these schemas, the component raises an error and Messaging Engine places the message in the suspended queue.

69. Which Interfaces do you need to implement in a general custom pipeline component?

A general pipeline component is a .NET or COM component that implements the following interfaces:

- IBaseComponent Interface
- IComponent Interface
- IComponentUI Interface
- And IPersistPropertyBag Interface.

A general pipeline component gets one message from the BizTalk Messaging Engine, processes it, and returns it to the BizTalk Server engine. General components can also be implemented so that they do not return messages to the server. Such components are called consuming components because the component receives messages but does not produce any result messages.

70. Which Interfaces do you need to implement in an assembling custom pipeline component?

An assembling component must implement the following interfaces:

- IBaseComponent
- IAssemblerComponent.
- IComponentUI.
- And IPersistPropertyBag.

71. Which Interfaces do you need to implement in a disassembling custom pipeline component?

A disassembling pipeline component receives one message on input and produces zero or more messages on output. Disassembling components are used to split interchanges of messages into individual documents. Disassembler components must implement the following interfaces:

- IBaseComponent.
- IDisassemblerComponent.
- IComponentUI.
- IPersistPropertyBag..

72. What is the IProbeMessgae interface used for?

Any pipeline component (general, assembling, or disassembling) can implement the **IProbeMessage** interface if it must support message probing functionality. A probing component is used in the pipeline stages that have **FirstMatch** execution mode. The **IProbeMessage** interface exposes a single method, **Probe**, which enables the component to check the beginning part of the message. The return value determines whether this component is run.

73. Where do you deploy custom pipeline components assembly?

All the .NET pipeline component assemblies (native and custom) must be located in the <installation directory>\Pipeline Components folder to be executed by the server. If the pipeline with a custom component will be deployed across several servers, the component's binaries must be present in the specified folder on every server. You do not need to add a custom pipeline component to be used by the BizTalk Runtime to the Global Assembly Cache (GAC). Custom COM components in the pipeline will also appear in the Toolbox, provided they are registered on the computer as a COM component. Custom .NET pipeline components must be placed into the <installation directory>\Pipeline Components folder.

74. How do you handle exceptions in BizTalk custom pipeline component?

That will depend on your custom pipeline component and what you intend to do with it. You can log the exception, and handle it by returning a valid message to next component. If you do not handle the error you can throw an exception where you set the error description. To report the name of the component that throws an error, set the Source property of the **Exception** object. The Messaging Engine uses the Message and Source properties of the **Exception** object to report an error. The following message is written to the event log:

"There was a failure executing the [receive|send] pipeline: <pipeline name> Source: <Source> [Receive Location|Send Port:] <location|port name> Reason: <Message>."

---

75. Can you call a pipeline form an orchestration?

Yes, but only BizTalk 2006 has the ability to synchronously call a pipeline from within an Orchestration. This enables orchestrations to leverage the message processing encapsulated within a pipeline (either send or receive) against a body of data without having to send that data through the messaging infrastructure. You can use this feature to enable an orchestration to call a send pipeline in order to aggregate several messages into a single outgoing interchange. Conversely, an orchestration could call a receive pipeline to decode and disassemble an interchange obtained outside of the messaging infrastructure, without incurring the processing costs of going through the message box. Orchestrations use methods in the **XLANGPipelineManager** class (in the **Microsoft.XLANGs.Pipeline** namespace) to call send or receive pipelines. A Receive pipeline consumes either a single message or an interchange and yields zero or more messages, just as when the pipeline executes in the context of receiving a message within BizTalk messaging. A Send pipeline consumes one or more messages and yields a single message or interchange, again, just as when the pipeline executes in the context of sending a message within BizTalk messaging.

---

76. How would you call a Receive Pipeline from an orchestration?

You can call a receive pipeline from within an orchestration by using the **ExecuteReceivePipeline()** method of the **XLANGPipelineManager** class. This method consumes a single interchange and returns a collection of zero or more messages (contained in an instance of the **ReceivePipelineOutputMessages** class). A call to a receive pipeline would typically be done in an Expression shape within the orchestration. You must reference the pipeline assembly in the orchestration project.

---

77. How would you call a Send Pipeline from and orchestration?

You can call a send pipeline from within an orchestration, the application calls the **ExecuteSendPipeline()** method of the **XLANGPipelineManager** class. This method consumes a collection of one or more messages (contained in an instance of the

SendPipelineInputMessages class) and returns a single interchange. Because execution of a send pipeline yields a new interchange, the call to **ExecuteSendPipeline()** method must be made within a message assignment shape. You must reference the pipeline assembly in the orchestration project.

---

78. How would you handle Failures in a pipeline called from and orchestration?

Any failure in pipeline execution which would have resulted in a suspended message will result in an exception being thrown. The exception thrown is of type **Microsoft.XLANGs.Pipeline.XLANGPipelineManagerException**. This exception can be handled in a catch block within the calling orchestration. If the orchestration does not catch the thrown exception, the **XLANGs** engine reports an error, the text of which includes the exception information in the thrown exception.

---

79. How would you debug a deployed Pipeline?

HAT and the event viewers provide useful information about message processing failures in deployed components -- information that can often be used to narrow down the source of a problem. Once a custom pipeline has been implicated, source level debugging can be used to identify any problematic code.

---

80. How would you debug a custom pipeline component?

To debug a Deployed Custom Pipeline using Visual Studio 2005

- Load the custom pipeline project solution into Visual Studio 2005.

- Change the output path for your solution to <Installation Folder>\Pipeline Components. In Solution Explorer, right-click your project, click the Build tab, and then change the Output Path by clicking the Browse button and selecting the <Installation Folder>\Pipeline Components directory.

- From within Visual Studio 2005, deploy the solution by clicking Build | Deploy.

- Restart the host instance that runs the pipeline. Using the BizTalk Server Management console, navigate to the host instance that runs the pipeline, right-click the host instance then click Restart.

- Attach the Visual Studio 2005 debugger to BTSNTSVC.exe. This can be done by clicking Debug | Attach to Process, click Show processes in all sessions, and then double-click on BTSNTSVC.exe.

- Set breakpoints.

- Drop a message in the appropriate location to initiate the custom pipeline component. Processing should halt on the breakpoints you set.

Maps Questions

81. What are the default functoids?

There are many out of the box functiods. They can be categorized as follows:

- Advanced: Assert, Index, Iteration, Looping, Mass Copy, Nil Value, Record Count, Scripting, Table Extractor, Table Looping, Value Mapping, Value Mapping (Flattening).

- Conversion: Used to convert to and from ASCII, and between numeric bases. ASCII to Character, Character to ASCII, Hexadecimal, Octal.

- Cumulative: Used to perform mathematical operations in looping records, such as averages and concatenation. Cumulative Average, Cumulative Concatenate, Cumulative Maximum, Cumulative Minimum, Cumulative Sum.

- Database: Used to extract data from a database and use it in destination instance messages. Database Lookup, Error Return, Format Message, Get Application ID, Get Application Value, Get Common ID, Get Common Value, Remove Application ID, Set Common ID, Value Extractor.

- Date and Time: Used to retrieve the current date and time, and to calculate delta times. Add Days, Date, Date and Time, Time.

- Logical: Used to perform a variety of logical operations, such as greater than and logical existence. Equal, Greater Than, Greater Than or Equal To, IsNil, Less Than, Less Than or Equal To, Logical AND, Logical Date, Logical Existence, Logical Numeric, Logical NOT, Logical OR, Logical String, Not Equal.

- Mathematical: Used to perform a variety of mathematical operations, such as addition and multiplication. Absolute Value, Addition, Division, Integer, Maximum Value, Minimum Value, Modulo, Multiplication, Round, Square Root, Subtraction.

- Scientific: Used to perform a variety of scientific operations, such as logarithms and trigonometry. 10^n, Arc Tangent, Base-Specified Logarithm, Common Logarithm, Cosine, Natural Exponential Function, Natural Logarithm, Sine, Tangent, X^Y.

- String: Used to perform a variety of string functions, such as trimming and concatenation. Lowercase, Size, String Concatenate, String Extract, String Find, String Left, String Left Trim, String Right, String Right Trim, Uppercase.

82. What does the Value Mapping Functoid do?

There are two flavors of the "Value Mapping Functiod". The regular Value Mapping functoid returns the value of its second parameter if its first parameter is true. A common use of the functoid is to change the attributes of a field into the attributes of a record. And, the flattening Value Mapping functoid which enables you to flatten a portion of an input instance message by converting multiple records into a single record.

83. What is a good way to arrange your Map?

Create several pages in the map, with each map corresponding to a different kind of mapping sophistication.

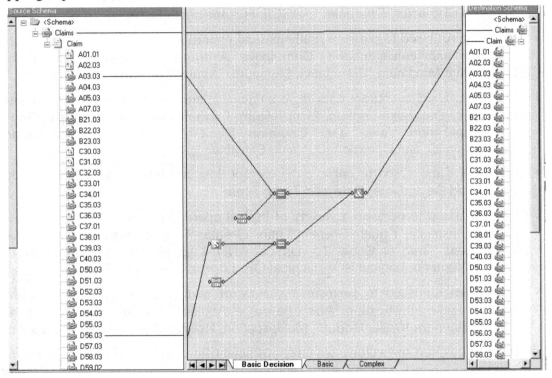

Figure 6: Sample Map

Figure 6 shows a map with several pages. In the first page, we have the "basic decision" to select the different records that would be mapped, a "basic" page that have the simple mappings, and a complex page that have complex mapping and scripts calls.

84. What does the Assert Functoid do?

The Assert functoid either outputs a string value or throws an exception based on a Boolean value.

85. What does the Iteration Functoid do?

The Iteration functoid outputs the index of the current record in a looping structure, starting at 1 for the first record, 2 for the second record, and so on.

86. What does the Mass Copy Functoid do?

The Mass Copy functoid enables your maps to use schemas that include any anyAttribute elements. These elements are wildcards provided in the XML Schema definition language to match unknown structures or attributes. The Mass Copy functoid copies the element in the input instance message corresponding to the source schema node connected to the Mass Copy functoid. The functoid also copies any and all of its substructure, and recreates it in the output instance message at the linked node in the destination schema. Thus, you can also use the Mass Copy functoid to copy any source and destination records having identical substructures.

87. What does the Table Looping Functoid do?

The Table Looping functoid enables you to create a table of output values to use in creating the output instance message. The data in the table can consist of links and constants.

88. What does the Table Extractor Functoid do?

The Table Extractor functoid determines which data to extract from each row of the looping grid as the Table Looping functoid presents the rows. You need one Table Extractor functoid for each output field.

89. What does the Scripting Functoid do?

The Scripting functoid enables you to use custom script or code at run time to perform functions otherwise not available. The Scripting functoid in supports the following languages:

- C# .NET
- JScript .NET
- Visual Basic .NET
- Extensible Stylesheet Language Transformations (XSLT)
- XSLT Call Templates

---

90. If you have many scripts that you want to put in a map how would you do that?

I would have the scripts in a separate assembly that I reference from the Maps assembly, and configure the scripting functiod to call the required script, as shown in Figure 7.

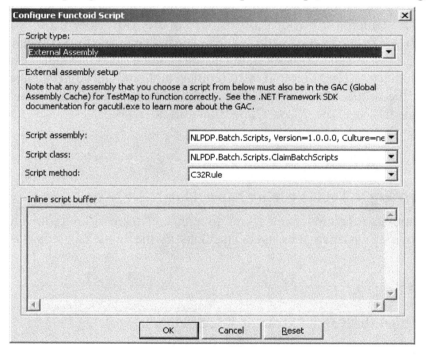

Figure 7: Sample Script Functiod calling an external script

This will allow the use of the same script in more than one map.

---

91. What is a link in a Map?

A link specifies the basic function of copying data from an element or attribute in an input instance message to an element or attribute in an output instance. You create links between records and fields in the source and destination schemas at design time. This drives the creation, at run time, of an output instance message conforming to the destination schema from an input instance message conforming to the source schema.

92. What are the important properties of a link in a Map?

- Source Links: You use the Source Links property to configure the nature of the data from an input instance message that will be used to construct the output instance message. The default, and most common choice, is to use the element or attribute value from the input instance message. Other choices are possible, including the use of the name of the element or attribute from the input instance message.

- Target Links: You use the Target Links property to configure how BizTalk **Mapper** will match node-hierarchy levels. By default, source schema hierarchies are flattened as the output instance message is created. You can also choose to have hierarchies preserved, matching links from either the top down or from the bottom up.

- Label: You use the Label property to create a more readable name for the link than the XPath value that is used by default. Configuring this property is especially helpful when the link is used as an input to a functiod.

93. If I have an XLST and I want to call it from an orchestration, what should I do?

You need to create an empty map and set its Custom XSLT Path grid property to your XSLT. If your XSLT code uses external .NET assemblies, you will also need to create a custom extension XML file. Use the Custom Extension XML property to open the Select Custom Extension XML File dialog box, in which you can select the file that contains the custom extension XML for the map.

94. How to implement a custom functiod?

To implement a custom functiod, you must derive your functiod from the **BaseFunctoid** class. You must first override the constructor and make a set of calls that tell BizTalk **Mapper** about your custom functiod. Then you need to write the functiod logic. You must perform a number of tasks in the class constructor override method to characterize your functiod. In addition to any functiod-specific code your solution requires, you need to perform the following tasks:

- Assign a unique ID to the functoid: Use a value greater than 6000 that has not been used. Values less than 6000 are reserved for use by internal functoids.

- Set HasSideEffects: HasSideEffects is used by the mapper to optimize the XSLT code that is generated. This property is true by default.

- Point to the resource assembly by calling the SetupResourceAssembly method.

- Set the following properties SetName, SetTooltip,SetDescription,SetBitmap

- Assign the functoid to one or more categories: by setting the Category property by using one or more FunctoidCategory values.

- Specify the number of parameters accepted. Use the SetMinParams method to set the number of required parameters and the SetMaxParams method to set the number of optional parameters.

- Declare what can connect to your functoid. Call AddInputConnectionType once for each ConnectionType that the functoid supports.

- Declare what your functoid can connect to by setting OutputConnectionType to tell BizTalk Mapper the types of objects that can receive output from your functoid. Use OR to specify multiple connection types.

- Tell BizTalk Server which methods to invoke for your functoid. For cumulative functoids, use SetExternalFunctionName to set the initialization function, SetExternalFunctionName2 to set the accumulation function, and SetExternalFunctionName3 to specify the function that returns the accumulated value. For noncumulative functoids use SetExternalFunctionName to set the functoid method.

- To allow BizTalk Server to use inline code to invoke your functoid. Call AddScriptTypeSupport with ScriptType to enable inline code. Invoke SetScriptBuffer to pass in the code for the functoid. This code will be copied into the map.

- Declare global variables for an inline functoid by using the SetScriptGlobalBuffer: this will make any declarations made will be visible to other inline scripts included in the map.

- Indicate which helper functions your inline functoid requires: Use values from the InlineGlobalHelperFunction enumeration to specify which helper functions are required. Use OR to specify multiple helper functions.

- Validate all the parameters passed to your functoid.

- Implementing Functoid Logic: To make the functoid useful you must implement one or more methods depending upon the functoid category. If the functoid is cumulative, then you need to supply three methods—the first for initialization, the second to do the accumulation, and the third to return the accumulated value. If the functoid is not cumulative, then you need to supply one method that returns a value.

- You also have to decide whether the functoid implementation code should be copied inline into the map, or kept within a compiled .NET assembly and used through a reference.
  - ○ Consider using an inline functoid when:
    - It is okay for others to read and potentially modify your business logic.
    - Your functoid depends only upon .NET Framework namespaces that the map supports.
    - You do not want to deploy and maintain another assembly with your BizTalk solution.
    - You are writing a series of functoids that share variables.
  - ○ Consider using a referenced functoid when:
    - You do not want your business logic copied into the map where it might be seen or modified by others.
    - Your functoid depends upon .NET Framework classes that the map does not support.
    - The added functionality provided by the .NET Framework justifies deploying and maintaining another assembly with your BizTalk solution.

Messaging Questions

95. What are the types of subscriptions in BizTalk?

In BizTalk Server, there are two types of subscriptions:

- An activation subscription indicates that a message that fulfills the subscription should activate, or create, a new instance of the subscriber when it is received.

- An instance subscription indicates that messages that fulfill the subscription should be routed to an already-running instance of the subscriber.

The difference between the two types of subscription at the information level is that an instance subscription includes the unique instance ID, stored in the subscription table in the master MessageBox database. When an orchestration instance or receive port completes processing, instance subscriptions are removed from the MessageBox, while activation subscriptions remain active as long as the orchestration or send port is enlisted.

96. What is Batching in BizTalk?

Batching is a serialized processing of a set of messages that allows for optimizations with respect to database round trips. A batch is a unit of atomic work; that is, it either all succeeds or all fails. If one operation in a batch succeeds but another operation fails, all the operations that make up the batch are invalidated and must be repeated.

97. What is the role of the receive adapter in message processing?

The receive adapter initiates the process of receiving messages by reading a stream of data and creating a message. The adapter creates a message (an implementation of the Microsoft.BizTalk.Message.Interop.IBaseMessage interface), adds a part to it (an implementation of the Microsoft.BizTalk.Message.Interop.IBasePart interface), and provides the stream of data as the part content. The adapter writes and promotes into the message context properties related to the location, adapter type, and others related to the adapter. After the message and its context have been created, the adapter passes the message to the Endpoint Manager. The message is then processed through the receive pipeline, which has been configured for the receive location. After the message has been processed by the pipeline, a map may be used to transform the message into the format desired before the Endpoint Manager publishes the message with the Message Agent.

98. What is the role of receive pipeline in message processing?

The pipeline processes the message content as well as message context. Message content is generally handled in the decoding, disassembling, and validating stages. On the other hand, message context can be handled in all stages. A pipeline, however, does not necessarily act on either the content or the context. The job of the disassembler is to process an incoming message from an adapter and disassemble it into smaller messages, and parse the message data. When an incoming message has many smaller messages, this is known as an interchange.

99. Can a flat file message be processed without a custom pipeline?

No. You have to develop a custom pipeline for a flat file message. A Pipeline's job is to convert any external format into XML, be it a flat file or EDI or anything else.

100.   What are un-typed messages? how does one create them?

A message created in BizTalk Orchestration is bound to a schema. This is a typed message. Un-typed messages are bound to System.Xml.XmlDocument.

101.   What is the difference between static, dynamic and direct binding?

A port binding is the configuration information that determines where and how a message will be sent or received. Depending on its type, a port binding might refer to physical locations, pipelines, or other orchestrations. There are three types of port binding for ports that receive messages:

- Static Binding: The port binding are specified and fixed throughout the execution of the application. The binding are specified either at design time or deployment time but they do not change during the course of the execution.

- Dynamic Bindings: the port bindings are changed during the execution of the application. For example, this can be done on the basis of the logic of the orchestration, a property of an incoming message, and then specified in the Expression shape, as shown in the following code:

  ```
  DynamicSendPort(Microsoft.XLANGs.BaseTypes.Address)=
  "mailtoMoustafa@MoustafaRefaat.com";
  ```

- Direct Binding: Direct bound ports are logical one-way or two-way ports in your orchestrations that are not explicitly bound to any physical ports. Direct bound ports allow you to have different communication patterns among your services. To implement direct binding, select the Direct port binding option in Orchestration Designer at design time. There are three types of direct bound ports:

- o MessageBox direct bound port.
- o Self-correlating direct bound port.
- o Partner orchestration direct bound port.

---

102.   How do you enable send port subscriptions in BizTalk?

A filter on the Send Port will enable subscriptions in BizTalk. You can set the filter on any of context promoted properties, such as the receive port name, or ant of the message promoted properties.

---

103.   What is a Message Type (i.e. BTS.MessageType)? , and how is it used in BizTalk?

When you create a schema to define the structure of messages, this schema defines the message type for that message. The type is determined by the root node and namespace in the schema definition. For example, an XML document that looks like the following:

```
<?xml version="1.0" encoding="utf-16"?>

<xs:schema xmlns="http://www.DIC.com/GSPI/FinanceFeedSchema"
xmlns:b="http://schemas.microsoft.com/BizTalk/2003"
targetNamespace="http://www.DIC.com/GSPI/FinanceFeedSchema"
xmlns:xs="http://www.w3.org/2001/XMLSchema">
 <xs:element name="DealFinancialInfo">
  <xs:annotation>
   <xs:appinfo>
    <b:recordInfo rootTypeName="DealFinancialInfo"
xmlns:b="http://schemas.microsoft.com/BizTalk/2003" />
   </xs:appinfo>
  </xs:annotation>
  <xs:complexType>
   <xs:sequence>
    <xs:element minOccurs="0" maxOccurs="unbounded" name="FeeInfo">
     <xs:complexType>
      <xs:sequence>
       <xs:element name="PrimaryBorrower">
        <xs:complexType>
         <xs:attribute name="FirstName" type="xs:string" />
         <xs:attribute name="MiddleName" type="xs:string" />
```

```
          <xs:attribute name="LastName" type="xs:string" />
       </xs:complexType>
     </xs:element>
     <xs:element name="Taxes">
      <xs:complexType>
        <xs:attribute name="Type" type="xs:string" />
        <xs:attribute name="Value" type="xs:string" />
      </xs:complexType>
     </xs:element>
     <xs:element name="Registeration">
      <xs:complexType>
        <xs:attribute name="Date" type="xs:string" />
        <xs:attribute name="Number" type="xs:string" />
        <xs:attribute name="Status" type="xs:string" />
        <xs:attribute name="Period" type="xs:string" />
      </xs:complexType>
     </xs:element>
    </xs:sequence>
    <xs:attribute name="ReportDate" type="xs:string" />
    <xs:attribute name="RequestDate" type="xs:string" />
    <xs:attribute name="ReferenceNumber" type="xs:string" />
    <xs:attribute name="PolicyNumber" type="xs:string" />
    <xs:attribute name="ProgramName" type="xs:string" />
    <xs:attribute name="ProgramType" type="xs:string" />
    <xs:attribute name="ColateralType" type="xs:string" />
    <xs:attribute name="DealType" type="xs:string" />
    <xs:attribute name="ProvinceCode" type="xs:string" />
    <xs:attribute name="SaleDate" type="xs:string" />
    <xs:attribute name="CancallationDate" type="xs:string" />
    <xs:attribute name="LenderBranch" type="xs:string" />
    <xs:attribute name="LoanNumber" type="xs:string" />
    <xs:attribute name="LoanAmount" type="xs:string" />
    <xs:attribute name="LiabilityAmount" type="xs:string" />
    <xs:attribute name="Recipient" type="xs:string" />
```

```
            <xs:attribute name="ServiceID" type="xs:string" />
            <xs:attribute name="FeeAmount" type="xs:string" />
            <xs:attribute name="FeeType" type="xs:string" />
            <xs:attribute name="LOB" type="xs:string" />
            <xs:attribute name="Division" type="xs:string" />
          </xs:complexType>
        </xs:element>
      </xs:sequence>
    </xs:complexType>
  </xs:element>
</xs:schema>
```

Would have a message type of

http://www.DIC.com/GSPI/FinanceFeedSchema# DealFinancialInfo

104.   What would you consider when promoting properties?

Before promoting a property into the message context, we should consider the following:

- Property size: To increase routing performance, promoted properties are limited to 255 characters. There is no limit to the size of properties that are simply written to the context. However, writing large properties to the message context will still decrease performance, as the Messaging Engine needs to process and manage the context regardless of how big it is.

- Performance: Large message properties cannot be "streamed" and must be entirely loaded into memory by the runtime. This will become an issue if you write large values for message properties into the message context..

- Overwriting of promoted properties: If you promote a property to the message context, and issue a context write operation, the property is no longer promoted.

- Dealing with Nulls: Null properties are not persisted to the context. If you set a property's value to Null, it will no longer exist, and you cannot see a context property in the HAT with a value of Null.

105.   How to enable failed Message routing in BizTalk 2006?

We need to ensure that any receive or send ports with error handling capabilities have the Generate Error Report option checked. This will signal the runtime engine to generate the routing failure message and publish it to the **MessageBox**. We can subscribe to all the messages that have http://schemas.microsoft.com/BizTalk/2005/error-report property set and we can handle all failure messages.

---

106.   What is Message suspension?

BizTalk Server stores messages associated with suspended pipelines in the MessageBox database. If a failure occurs in the pipeline, BizTalk Server suspends the instance of a message. Not all instances of suspended service can be resumed. This depends on the cause of suspension. BizTalk Server does not automatically remove suspended instances that you cannot resume from the MessageBox database. You can choose to save a service instance to disk before removing it from the suspended queue.

---

107.   What are the Message Failure Points that would cause the message to be suspended?

A message may fail in the message processing engine in one of the stages defined below resulting in the entire Interchange being suspended:

- Validate stage
- Resolve Party stage
- During Mapping

Recoverable Interchanges do not allow for recovery from map failures. If a BizTalk map fails during an Interchange, the entire Interchange stops processing, even if RIP is enabled. Interchanges that fail processing due to one of these errors will become suspended. These Interchanges can then be resumed from within the BizTalk Administration Console. However, the Interchange will still likely fail unless the underlying cause of the failure is addressed. Interchange processing will stop within the XMLDisassembler component if the message data is not well-formed XML. Since the data is read as a stream, a good check is to see whether document properties that would cause System.Xml.XmlReader to error are present. If they are, the XMLDisassembler will also fail. Messages that are extracted from Interchanges but fail because of a "No matching subscription found" error can be successfully resumed. All that is needed in this case is to ensure the BizTalk port or orchestration that has a subscription for the message is enlisted.

---

108.   How to route binary data?

To route binary data you can use pass-through pipelines on the receive location and send port. BizTalk will route (copy) the data from the source (receive location) to the destination (send port). If you want to route the binary data based on some information in

---

the binary data then you write a custom Disassembler to promote the properties you need from the incoming message to route the binary data.

109. How to reorder messages that are arriving out of order?

You can do so either by using the "Ordered Delivery" feature that is available for a port inside an orchestration, or within a messaging port. The "Ordered Delivery" forces the port to deliver the messages out of the MessageBox in the order in which they were received. This ensures that the first-in first-out pattern is followed when dealing with message arriving on a port. However, the ordered Delivery feature might cause performance issues. This is because BizTalk engine will single-thread each of the messages as they arrive on the port to their appropriate destination. And Ordered Delivery assumes that the messages arrive in the correct order. If the messages are not arriving in the correct order you have to implement the Resequencer pattern.

110. How to Edit and resubmit suspended messages?

To Edit and resubmit a suspended message you first have to get the suspended message. You can use WMI to subscribe to MSBTS_ServiceInstanceSuspendedEvent and call the SaveToFile method, which will allow you access to the suspended message and its context. You can then use WMI to remove the message from the suspended queue. Editing the message after that is a matter of your choice. When the errors are frequent and predictable, then you might be able to write a custom parsing tool that would fix these messages. Or you can use your favorite text or xml editor to edit the message and fix it directly. To resubmit the message, you can add another receive location to the same receive port where the message was originally sent. Another option is to use a third party tool like BT Error Manager from **WWW.BizTalkGear.Com** to manage the errors on the whole server. This provides a more cost effective solution. Or if your project has a big budget you can use MOM and develop lots of code to do the above.

111. Can we publish orchestrations and schemas as WCF services?

Yes. BizTalk Server 2006 R2 provides the BizTalk WCF Service Publishing Wizard and the BizTalk WCF Service Consuming Wizard. You can use the BizTalk WCF Service Publishing Wizard to create and publish BizTalk orchestrations as WCF services, and to publish schemas as WCF services. You can use the BizTalk WCF Service Consuming Wizard to generate BizTalk Server artifacts, such as orchestrations and types, to consume a WCF service based on the metadata document of the WCF service.

BizTalk Adapters and Accelerators Questions

112.   What are the out-of-box BizTalk Adaptors?

The Default Adapters are:

- File: Easy to use handling access to files on local or shared folders

- FTP: Supports FTP protocol.

- HTTP(s): Supports the HTTP and HTTPS protocols

- SOAP: Supports the SOAP protocol for the use of Web services.

- MSMQT: Supports guaranteed once-only delivery of messages between BizTalk Server and Microsoft Message Queuing.

- MSMQ: Supports guaranteed once-only delivery of messages between BizTalk Server and Microsoft Message Queuing.

- MQ Series: Supports guaranteed once-only delivery of messages between BizTalk Server and IBM WebSphere MQ for Windows platforms.

- SQL: Supports direct communication between BizTalk Server and SQL Server databases.

- Windows SharePoint Services: Supports the use of Windows SharePoint Services.

- POP3: Supports receiving documents through e-mail.

- SMTP: Supports sending documents through e-mail.

- EDI: Supports processing of business documents that conform to the EDI standard.

- WCF-WSHttp: Supports WS-* standards over the HTTP transport.

- WCF-BasicHttp: Communicates with ASMX-based Web services and clients and other services that conform to the WS-I Basic Profile 1.1 using HTTP or HTTPS.

- WCF-NetTcp: Supports WS-* standards over the TCP transport.

- WCF-NetMsmq: Supports queuing by leveraging Microsoft Message Queuing (MSMQ) as a transport.

- WCF-NetNamedPipe: Provides a fast transport for cross-process communication on the same machine (only for WCF apps).

- WCF-Custom: Enables the use of WCF extensibility features.

- WCF-CustomIsolated: Enables the use of WCF extensibility features over the HTTP transport.

Line of Business Adapters

Following is a list of the Line of Business (LOB) adapters provided by Microsoft. These adapters are downloaded separately:

- SAP: Enables exchange of Intermediate Document (IDOC), BAPI, and Request for Comments (RFC) messages between BizTalk Server and an SAP R/3 system. SAP R/3 4.x and R/3 6.20 (Enterprise).

- PeopleSoft Enterprise: Enables exchange of Component Interface (CI) messages between BizTalk Server and a PeopleSoft system. 8.17.02, 8.43, and 8.45

- JD Edwards OneWorld XE: Enables exchange of Business Function messages between BizTalk Server and a JD Edwards OneWorld system. B7.3.3.3 with SP23

- JD Edwards EnterpriseOne: Enables exchange of Business Function messages between BizTalk Server and a JD Edwards EnterpriseOne system. 8.10

- ODBC Adapter for Oracle Database: Enables reading and writing information from and to an Oracle Server database. 8i (8.1.6.0), 9i (9.2.0.1), or 10i

- Siebel eBusiness Applications: Enables exchange of Business Components and Business Service messages between BizTalk Server and a Siebel eBusiness Application. 6.2.1 with patch 110 or higher, 7.0.3, 7.5.2, 7.7 and 7.8

- TIBCO Rendezvous: Enables exchange of XML and binary data format messages between BizTalk Server and TIBCO Rendezvous. 7.3

- TIBCO Enterprise Message Service: Enables exchange of XML and binary data format messages between BizTalk Server and a TIBCO EMS server providing a tightly integrated and reliable application infrastructure. 4.2

- WebSphere MQ: Enables exchange of messages between BizTalk Server and IBM WebSphere MQ. 5.3 with Fix Pack 10 or higher and 6.0 with Fix Pack 1 or higher

- Web Services Enhancements (WSE) 2.0: Enables more secure Web services (WS-Security, WS-Trust, WS-SecureConversation, WS-SecurityPolicy, and WS-Policy) with BizTalk Server 2004. Download WSE Service Pack 1 to use this adapter with BizTalk Server 2006.

---

113.   What are the BizTalk Adapter Message Exchange Patterns?

The BizTalk Adapter Framework supports a rich set of message exchange patterns that adapters can use in many powerful messaging scenarios.

- One-Way (Asynchronous): The key concept here is that messages flow in one direction.

- Request-Response Style Protocols (Sync-on-Async): A request-response scenario consists of receiving a request message, processing it, and sending a response message.

- Solicit-Response Style Protocols: This scenario is initiated by sending a solicit message and completed by receiving a response message. It is referred to as solicit-response because the initial message sent is soliciting an endpoint for a response message.

- Request-Multiresponse: This scenario is similar to the request-response scenario. However, in this scenario multiple responses may be returned for a given request.

- Loop-Back: This scenario is similar to the request-response scenario. The request message is published as usual, but the engine ensures that the response message is routed back to the same adapter instance that published the request message. Because the request message is published to the MessageBox database, the tracking infrastructure ensures that both the request and response messages are tracked. This is also a good way to invoke a send pipeline processing on message then immediately get the output message sent back to the adapter for subsequent processing.

114.   What interface do you need to implement to develop a BizTalk Adapter?

All adapters must implement the following interfaces.

- IBaseComponent: This interface details the Name, Version, and Description of the adapter.

- IBTTransport: This interface details the Transport Type and ClassID of the adapter.

- IBTBatchCallback: This interface is a callback interface through which the adapter receives status and error information for a batch of messages it submits to the Messaging Engine.

- IPersistPropertyBag(optional): This is a configuration interface through which handler configuration is delivered to the adapter. This interface is required only for adapters that have handler configuration information.

- IBTTransportControl(optional):This interface is used to initialize and terminate an adapter. The adapter's transport proxy is passed to it through this interface. This interface is not required for isolated adapters.

115.   What are the Adapter Hosting Models?

In general BizTalk adapters are hosted in the BizTalk service, **Btsntsvc.exe**. This means that BizTalk Server manages the lifetime of the adapter.

- In-Process Adapters: Adapters that are managed by BizTalk Server are called in-process adapters. BizTalk Server does the following for these adapters:

    o   Instantiate the adapter when BizTalk Server is started

    o   Passes the adapter's transport proxy to the adapter during initialization

    o   Services the adapter's requests

    o   Terminates the adapter on shutdown of the BizTalk Server service

- Isolated Adapters: There are scenarios when hosting receive adapters in the BizTalk service are not possible. For example, the Internet Information Services (IIS) process model is such that IIS manages the lifetime of ASP.NET applications and ISAPI extensions. The BizTalk SOAP adapter must run within the same process space as IIS, thus making it impossible for BizTalk Server to control the lifetime of any instances of the SOAP adapter. For these types of adapters there is another hosting model referred to as isolated receive adapters, or simply isolated adapters. There is no concept of an isolated send adapter. Because BizTalk Server cannot create an isolated adapter, the adapter must acquire its own transport proxy and register itself with that transport proxy.

116.   What are the components you will need to develop for a custom adapter?

A custom adapter shares the standardized configuration, management, and setup mechanisms used by the native adapters. With the standardization to the Adapter Framework, a custom adapter is managed by using the BizTalk Server Administration console. You will need to provide the following:

- Adapter Registry File: Certain information about adapters must be registered in the registry and the BizTalk Management database. Information such as an adapter's alias, receive handler, receive location, and transport type is called metadata.

- Design-Time Component: The user interface (UI) for a custom adapter is implemented by using the Adapter Framework. This is a productive approach to UI development because the UI is rendered from an XML schema provided as part of the adapter's assembly. A small amount of code is required to transform the contents of the schema into a UI to configure the adapter's properties.

- Run-Time Component: Typically an adapter consists of two public run-time components: the component that implements the message receiver and the component that implements the message sender. These components may be deployed in the same assembly or in two different assemblies.

- o Receive Adapter: A receive adapter is responsible for creating a new BizTalk message by attaching the network/data source stream to the message body. It also adds any metadata pertinent to the endpoint over which the data was received, and then submits that message to the Messaging Engine. The adapter deletes the data from the receive endpoint or sends the appropriate acknowledgment message to the client indicating that the data was accepted into BizTalk Server.

- o Send Adapter: A send adapter is responsible for sending a BizTalk message to the specified endpoint using its specific transport protocol.

117. How to add the SQL Adapter Schemas to a BizTalk Orchestration?

The Adapter Framework provides auto generation feature to add adapter schemas to BizTalk projects. You need to select a SQL server to connect to, and then you enter the information used to generate the schema. When the wizard is completed, two schemas are added to the BizTalk project if a send port is used, and one schema is added to the project if a receive port is used.

118. Do you need to modify the SQL Stored procedures to use SQL adapter?

Yes. This is because the SQL adapter uses SQLXML to render result sets as XML; the "for xml auto" clause should be included in the SELECT statement. While generating schemas for stored procedures you have to add ", type , xmldata." at the end of the SELECT statement. The type would generate a schema, and XMLData would allow SQL server to return more than the 2000 character strings.

119. What are the best practices for the FTP Adapter?

- Delete partially received files from the temporary folder on a regular basis to keep files from using computer resources and potentially disrupting service.

- When working with a streaming server, deny read access to the new file until the MessageBox database receives the entire file. If a partial file is submitted to the MessageBox database by the FTP adapter, the MessageBox database will successfully store the message, but the FTP adapter will not be able to delete the partial message from the receive location.

- To ensure high availability for the FTP adapter receive handler, the FTP adapter receive handler should be configured to run in a clustered BizTalk Host instance.

120.   What are the WCF Adapters?

The BizTalk Adapters for Windows Communication Foundation (WCF) allow Microsoft BizTalk Server 2006 R2 to communicate with WCF-based applications. The BizTalk WCF adapters are:

- WCF-WSHttp adapter. Provides the WS-* standards support over the HTTP transport. The WCF-WSHttp adapter implements the following specifications: WS-Transaction for the transactional interactions between external applications and the MessageBox database, and WS-Security for message security and authentication. The transport is HTTP or HTTPS, and message encoding is a Text or Message Transmission Optimization Mechanism (MTOM) encoding.

- WCF-BasicHttp adapter. Communicates with ASMX-based Web services and clients and other services that conform to the WS-I Basic Profile 1.1. The transport is HTTP or HTTPS, and message encoding is a text encoding.

- WCF-NetTcp adapter. Provides the WS-* standards support over the TCP transport. The WCF-NetTcp adapter provides efficient communication in a WCF-to-WCF environment. The adapter implements the following specifications: WS-Transaction for the transactional interactions between external applications and the MessageBox database, and WS-Security for message security and authentication. The transport is TCP, and message encoding is binary encoding.

- WCF-NetMsmq adapter. Provides support for queuing by leveraging Microsoft Message Queuing (MSMQ) as a transport and enables support for loosely coupled applications, failure isolation, load leveling, and disconnected operations.

- WCF-NetNamedPipe adapter. Provides secure optimization for on-machine cross-process communication. The WCF-NetNamedPipe adapter uses transport security for transfer security, named pipes for message delivery, and binary message encoding.

- WCF-Custom adapter. Enables the use of WCF extensibility features. The adapter allows you to select and configure a WCF binding and the behavior information for the receive location and send port.

- WCF-CustomIsolated adapter. Enables the use of WCF extensibility features over the HTTP transport. The adapter allows you to select and configure a WCF binding and the behavior information for the receive location running in an isolated host.

Orchestrations Questions

121. How do you handle Exceptions in BizTalk orchestration?

I will put the code that might cause an exception in a scope. Create an exception handler for the appropriate exception. If the exception handler completes normally, control passes to the surrounding scope. If no exception has been thrown in the surrounding scope, the orchestration continues to run. If the exception handler ends with a **throw** statement, the original exception is thrown again for the surrounding scope to act upon, unless you specify a different exception that you want to be thrown. If no exception handler can be located, the default exception handler will run. The default exception handler for a scope will call the compensations for any nested transactions.

122. What is Compensation?

If an error occurs and you need to undo or reverse the effects of a successfully committed transaction, you can do so by adding compensation code to your orchestration. The compensation can be invoked after the transaction has completed its actions successfully. At that point, the state of the orchestration is known, and state information is available to the code in the compensation, which means that you can write code to act appropriately depending on the state of the orchestration when the transaction commits. Compensations can also be provided on atomic transactions. These compensations can only be called after the atomic transaction commits. You need to write code to undo or reverse the path of the normal execution in the compensation. The compensation block is flexible; it can contain any other shape, including another transaction scope.

123. What is a scope?

A **scope** is a framework for grouping actions. It is primarily used for transactional execution and exception handling. A scope can contain one or more blocks. It has a body, and can optionally have appended to it any number of **exception-handling blocks**. It may have an optional compensation block as well, depending on the nature of the scope. A transactional scope will also have a default exception handler, and any number of additional exception handlers that you create for it. You can specify that scopes are **synchronized** or not synchronized. By synchronizing a scope, you ensure that any shared data accessed within the scope will not be over-written by any parallel action in your orchestration, nor will it be over-written while another action is reading it. **Atomic transaction scopes** are always synchronized. All actions within a **synchronized scope** are considered synchronized as well as all actions in any of its exception handlers. Actions in the compensation handler for a transactional scope are not synchronized. You can nest Scope shapes inside other scope shapes. You can also declare variables such as messages and correlation sets at the scope level. You cannot use the same name of a scope variable for an orchestration variable.

---

124. **What are the shapes that you can have in an orchestration?**

- **Call Orchestration:** Enables your orchestration to call another orchestration synchronously.

- **Call Rules:** Enables you to configure a Business Rules policy to be executed in your orchestration.

- **Compensate:** Enables you to call code to undo or compensate for operations already performed by the orchestration whenever an error occurs.

- **Construct Message:** Enables you to construct a message.

- **Decide:** Enables you to conditionally branch in your orchestration.

- **Delay:** Enables you to build delays in your orchestration based on a time-out interval.

- **Expression:** Enables you to assign values to variables or make .NET calls.

- **Group:** Enables you to group operations into a single collapsible and expandable unit for visual convenience.

- **Listen:** Enables your orchestration to conditionally branch depending on messages received or the expiration of a timeout period.

- **Loop:** Enables your orchestration to loop until a condition is met.

- **Message Assignment:** Enables you to assign message values.

- **Parallel Actions:** Enables your orchestration to perform two or more operations independently of each other.

- **Port:** Defines where and how messages are transmitted.

- **Receive:** Enables you to receive a message in your orchestration.

- ♨ **Role Link**: Enables you to create a collection of ports that communicate with the same logical partner, perhaps through different transports or endpoints.

- ▣ **Scope**: Provides a framework for transactions and exception handling.

- ✉ **Send**: Enables you to send a message from your orchestration.

- ▣ **Start Orchestration**: Enables your orchestration to call another orchestration asynchronously.

- ▣ **Suspend**: Suspends the operation of your orchestration to enable intervention in the event of some error condition.

- ▣ **Terminate**: Enables you to immediately end the operation of your orchestration in the event of some error condition.

- ▣ **Throw Exception**: Enables you to explicitly throw an exception in the event of an error.

- ▣ **Transform**: Enables you to map the fields from existing messages into new messages.

---

125. What are the transaction types in an orchestration?

- **Atomic Transactions**: BizTalk orchestrations can be designed to run discrete pieces of work, following the classic 'ACID' concept of a transaction.

- **Long-Running Transactions**: Long-running transactions provide custom scope-based compensation, custom scope-based exception handling, and the ability to nest transactions, all of which give you great flexibility in designing robust transaction architecture. You use a long-running transaction when the transaction might need to run for an extended time and you do not need full ACID properties (that is, you do not need to guarantee isolation of data from other transactions). A long-running transaction might have long periods of inactivity, often due to waiting for external messages to arrive.

---

126. When does the orchestration engine persist an orchestration state?

The orchestration engine saves the entire state of an orchestration instance at various persistence points to allow rehydration of the orchestration instance. The state includes any .NET-based components that may be used in the orchestration, in addition to messages and variables. The engine stores state at the following persistence points:

- End of a transactional scope (atomic or long running).
- At debugging breakpoints.
- At the execution of other orchestrations through the Start Orchestration shape.
- At the Send shape (except in an atomic transaction).
- When an Orchestration Instance is suspended.
- When the system shutdowns in a controlled manner.
- When the engine determines it wants to dehydrate.
- When an orchestration instance is finished.

127. Do all .Net based objects used in an orchestration have to be serializable?

No. But, in general, any .NET-based objects you use in orchestrations, either directly or indirectly, must be marked as serializable, unless they are invoked in atomic scopes, or if the objects are stateless and are invoked only through static methods. System.Xml.XmlDocument is a special case and does not need to be marked as serializable regardless of the transaction property for a scope.

128. Can we define Transactions on an Orchestration level?

Yes. Orchestrations can be transactional; an orchestration can itself be considered a scope. If the Transaction Type property for your orchestration is set to long-running or atomic, you can also select a value for the Compensation property, which can be Default or Custom.

129. Can we get messages to Orchestration without using (a or the) schema?

You can pass an XMLDocument to an orchestration; however this is highly discouraged as it can introduce bugs and issues to your solution.

130. What is dehydration, rehydration?

- Dehydration is the process of serializing the state of an orchestration into a SQL Server database. Dehydration is used to minimize the use of system resources by reducing the number of orchestrations that have to be instantiated in memory at one time.

- Rehydration is the reverse of this process. It is deserializing the last running state of an orchestration from the database.

131. When dehydration occurs?

The orchestration engine might determine that an orchestration instance has been idle for a relatively long period. It calculates thresholds to determine how long it will wait for various actions to take place, and if those thresholds are exceeded, it dehydrates the instance. This can occur under the following circumstances:

- When the orchestration is waiting to receive a message and the wait is longer than a threshold determined by the engine.

- When the orchestration is "listening" for a message, as it does when you use a Listen shape, and no branch is triggered before a threshold determined by the engine. The only exception to this is when the Listen shape contains an activation receive.

- When a delay in the orchestration is longer than a threshold determined by the engine.

- Between retries of an atomic transaction.

132. What is the cost of parallel shapes?

The use of parallel branches in orchestrations does not mean that these branches will run on parallel threads. It is simply an indication to the XLANG engine that operations in these branches may be interleaved, if necessary! The engine then makes the decision to run them on separate threads or interleave them. The engine decides whether new threads need to be allocated to perform the parallel branches and implements a persistence point before the parallel action, then one at the ending synchronization point. There is also the risk of corrupting data, as interleaved data access from multiple parallel branches might lead to unexpected behavior and undesirable values. To avoid data corruption, the logic accessing data should be encapsulated within synchronized scopes. Synchronized scopes will ensure that the data is being accessed by one thread or branch at a time. Using synchronized scopes will result in parallel branches being blocked on each other to ensure data integrity. This will slow down execution to ensure the predictability of the outcome. Depending on how complex and interdependent the logic is, it might be simpler to serially perform the data access instead of using parallel actions.

133.   Does the parallel shape provide parallel processing?

No. Activities that you put in parallel branches will still execute one at a time. However, they will not have to execute in any specific order. i.e. a process involving steps A, B, C could execute as BCA or CAB or ABC. What the parallel shape is referring to is a parallel activity in a business process and not a parallel activity in your computer program. The parallel shape isn't designed to instruct the system to run multiple threads, it is designed to allow multiple business activities to occur independently of each other without one having to wait for the other to complete.

134.   What is correlation?

Correlation is the process of matching an incoming message with the appropriate instance of an orchestration.

135.   What are the correlation exchange patterns?

There are three correlated messages exchange patterns:

- Traditional handshake: handshakes exist between the exchanges of the messages among the orchestrations or business processes. You can achieve the handshakes by defining correlation sets in the orchestrations where a correlation set is a list of promoted properties with specific values that you use to route messages to a specific orchestration instance.

- Sequential convoy: is a set of related messages that have a predefined order. Although the messages do not have to be exactly the same, BizTalk Server must receive them in a sequential order.

- Parallel convoy: enables multiple single messages to join together to achieve a required result. The set of related messages can arrive in any order, but BizTalk Server must receive all of them before starting the process.

136.   What are the types of correlation?

- Manual correlation: you manually configure the orchestrations to initialize and follow the correlation set to associate the messages with proper instances.

- Automatic correlation: the messaging engine will correlate the messages with the instances for you

137. What are zombies?

- A zombie message is a message that was routed to a running orchestration from the **MessageBox** and was "in flight" when the orchestration ended. An "in flight" message is a message that has been routed to a service instance and so is in a **MessageBox** queue destined for the service instance. Since the message can no longer be consumed by the subscribing orchestration instance, the message is suspended and marked with a **ServiceInstance**/State value of "Suspended (Non-resumable)".

- A zombie service instance is an instance of an orchestration which has completed while a message that was routed to the orchestration instance from the **MessageBox** was still "in flight". Since the orchestration instance has ended, it cannot consume the "in flight" messages and so is suspended and marked with a **ServiceInstance**/State value of "Suspended (Non-resumable)".

---

138. What causes zombies?

- Terminate control messages: The orchestration engine allows the use of control messages to cancel all currently running work in a specific orchestration instance. Since the control message immediately halts the running orchestration, zombie instances are not unexpected. A number of Human Workflow related designs tend to use this mechanism as well as some other designs.

- Parallel listen receives: In this scenario the service instance waits for 1-of-n messages and when it receives certain messages, it does some work and terminates. If messages are received on a parallel branch, just as the service instance is terminating, zombies are created.

- Sequential convoys with non-deterministic endpoints: In this scenario, a master orchestration schedule is designed to handle all messages of a certain type in order to meet some type of system design requirement. These design requirements may include ordered delivery, resource dispenser, and batching. For this case, the tendency is to define a while-loop surrounding a listen with one branch having a receive, and the other having a delay shape, followed by some construct, which sets some variable to indicate that the while loop should stop. This is non-deterministic, since the delay could be triggered, but a message could still be delivered. Non-deterministic endpoints similar to this are prone to generating zombies.

139.   How would you know that there are zombies in your BizTalk Solution?

When a zombie service instance is suspended in Microsoft BizTalk Server 2006 the following error message is generated:" 0xC0C01B4C The instance completed without consuming all of its messages. The instance and its unconsumed messages have been suspended". In BizTalk Server 2004 is "Completed With Discarded Messages".

---

140.   What is the difference between a delay shape and a listen shape?

A 'Delay' is very much similar to a "sleep" on the current thread. You can use System.DateTime, which causes your orchestration to pause until the specified date and time is reached. Or, you can use System.TimeSpan, which causes your orchestration to pause for the specified length of time.

Listen shape enable applications to wait for one of several messages on one or more ports, or to stop waiting after a specified time-out interval, and branch based upon the results.

---

141.   When you use Call Orchestration shape versus Start Orchestration shape?

You use "Call Orchestration" shape to synchronously call another orchestration. When you invoke another nested orchestration synchronously, the enclosing orchestration waits for the nested orchestration to finish before continuing.

You use "Start Orchestration" to invoke another orchestration asynchronously, that is, the flow of control in the invoking orchestration proceeds beyond the invocation, without waiting for the invoked orchestration to finish its work.

---

142.   How do you implement dynamic parallel orchestrations?

The Parallel Actions shape allows only for a static number of branches in design mode. You can use the "Start Orchestration" shape in a loop to start a dynamic number of execution paths in runtime.

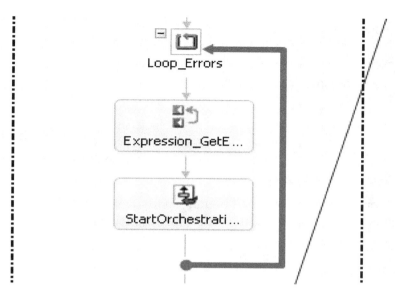

Figure 8: Sample starting orchestrations in a loop

Figure 8 shows this pattern.

---

143. What are Role Links in Orchestrations?

Role links are a form of abstraction for the interactions between your orchestration and your trading partners. Role links enable you to dynamically choose which trading partner to interact with based on trading partner resolution, message content, or the results of a database lookup while maintaining your overall business process intact.

---

144. What are Role Types in Orchestrations?

There are two roles in an orchestration:

- An "implements" role to receive and process messages. This role is also known as the provider.

- A "uses" role to send messages. This role is also known as the consumer.

---

145. What are the Direct Bound Port types in Orchestrations?

- **MessageBox** direct bound ports allow for publish-subscribe design patterns. Messages sent on a **MessageBox** direct bound port are published to the **MessageBox** database, where message recipients pick them up based on subscriptions. Logical receive ports configured as **MessageBox** direct bound ports get messages directly from the **MessageBox** database. For activating Receive shapes, the **MessageBox** direct bound receive ports get the messages through subscriptions to the message type and the filter expression. For non-activating Receive shapes, the **MessageBox** direct bound receive ports get the messages through subscriptions to the message type and the correlation set.

- Self-correlating direct bound ports assist you in designing asynchronous inter-orchestration communication. Messages sent to a self-correlating direct bound port are routed to the instance of the orchestration that created the receiving end of the self-correlated direct bound port.

- Partner orchestration direct bound ports provide for inter-orchestration communication. Messages sent on a partner orchestration direct bound port can be sent to an intended recipient orchestration, and messages received on a partner orchestration direct bound port can be received from an intended sender orchestration.

146. How to expose an Orchestration as a web-service?

You use the BizTalk Web Services Publishing Wizard to publish an orchestration as a Web service. The wizard creates a Web service based on an orchestration in a BizTalk assembly. Using the wizard, you select orchestrations and receive ports to publish Web services. You can define target namespaces, SOAP header requirements, and locations for the Web service project the wizard generates.

147. How to consume a web service?

You can consume (call) a Web service from your orchestration using Web ports. To consume a Web service from an orchestration, you create a Web port and construct Web messages. When you add a Web reference to your project, BizTalk creates an orchestration Web port type, Web message types, Reference.map (map file), Reference.odx (orchestration file), <WebService>.disco (discovery file), and <WebService>.wsdl (Web Service Description Language file) in the project. If your Web Service Description Language (WSDL) file contains schema Web message types, BizTalk adds Reference.xsd to the project. When you add a Web reference, all the Web methods for that Web service must be compatible with BizTalk Server.

148. If I am planning to expose an orchestration as BPEL, can I call web services from that same orchestration?

No. When you reference a Web reference from an existing BizTalk project, the BPEL export process will auto-generate a second WSDL file, and you will lose the binding information

---

149. How to debug an orchestration?

BizTalk Health and Activity Tracking (HAT) is a debugging tool that enables you to trace, view, and report on high-level progress, or low-level details of your business process and the components that implement it. In addition, you can debug your orchestrations by writing the information to the event log to trace the output or using custom code to track the business process.

You can use HAT to query a suspended instance, resume the instance in debug mode, and add appropriate breakpoints using the Technical Details View. This will enable you to trace the activities and debug messages step by step. To perform interactive debugging of an orchestration in HAT, you must deploy and execute at least one instance of the orchestration you want to debug. To do so, you will have to perform the following steps:

- Deploy and execute the orchestration you want to debug at least once. This will generate an instance of the orchestration that you can attach to in HAT. Without this step, HAT will not know about your orchestration and will not have a way to display it.

- View the orchestration in the Orchestration Debugger by executing one of the canned queries or by running a custom query. This exposes the orchestration so that you can set class-level breakpoints.

- Set a class-level breakpoint on the orchestration shapes you are interested in debugging. Future instances of the orchestration will break at the shapes specified.

- Generate one or more new orchestration instances by submitting appropriate messages. You should use messages that exercise the appropriate shapes in the orchestration. For example, if you have a decision shape, make sure your sample message will trigger the branch you are interested in.

- Attach to the orchestration instance by using Debug | Attach.

- Review variable names and values including message part contents.

- Resume the orchestration. If no more breakpoints are encountered, the debugger will detach from the instance.

- Remove class-level breakpoints.

150. **What is the difference between a "Message Assignment" shape and an "Expression" shape?**

A "Message Assignment" shape is used to create a new message and assign values to it. An Expression shape is used to assign values to variables or call other .Net Assemblies.

---

151. **Does BizTalk Orchestrations support recursion?**

Not directly. You can submit a message from the same orchestration that will cause it to restart start. But be cautious, as this might lead to infinite loop. You must have some condition or logic to stop the resubmition.

---

152. **What is the purpose of the property "Activate" in a Receive shape?**

If you set the Activate property to True, the runtime engine will test an incoming message to see whether it is of the right type, a filter has been applied, or the filter expression is satisfied. If the criteria for receipt of the message are met, the runtime engine creates and runs a new orchestration instance, and the Receive shape receives the message.

---

153. **Can an orchestration Start without an Activatable receive?**

Yes. But remember that an orchestration must have at least one receive shape with activate set to true or has the parameters defined for the orchestration.

---

154. **When do we need set the property "Synchronized" = true for a scope?**

This needs to be set, when variables are shared across the branches of a parallel shape, and you need to keep them synchronized.

Rules Engine Questions

155. What is business rule?

A **business rule** is a statement that defines or constrains some aspect of the business. It is intended to assert a business structure, to control, or influence the behavior of the business. A business rule is a declarative statement that governs the conduct of business processes. In BizTalk, a rule consists of a condition and actions. The condition is evaluated, and if it evaluates to true, the rule engine initiates one or more actions. Rules in the Business Rules Framework are defined by using the "IF condition THEN action" format.

156. What is a Policy?

A **policy** is a logical grouping of rules. You compose a version of a policy, save it, test it by applying it to facts, and when you are satisfied with the results, publish it and deploy it to a production environment. After you have defined all the rules in your policy, you can publish the policy version. In this way the policy is locked, and its behavior is well-defined.

157. What are Vocabularies?

A **vocabulary** is a collection of definitions consisting of friendly names for the facts used in rule conditions and actions. Vocabulary definitions make the rules easier to read, understand, and share by people in a particular business domain.

158. What are Facts?

Facts are discrete pieces of information about the world. Facts can originate from many sources (event systems, objects in business applications, database tables, and so on), and must be fed into the Business Rule engine using one of the following elements:

- .NET objects (methods, properties, and fields): you can specify a .NET assembly as a data source. You can subsequently select a class or class member from the assembly, and drag it onto a vocabulary definition or rule.

- XML documents (elements, attributes, and document subsections)

- Database rowsets (values from table column).

159.   What are Typed Facts?

Typed facts are classes that implement the ITypedFact interface: TypedXmlDocument, DataConnection, TypedDataTable, and TypedDataRow.

- TypedXmlDocument: The TypedXmlDocument class represents the XML document type in the Business Rules Framework. When you use a node of an XML document as an argument in a rule, two XPath expressions are created: the Selector, and the Field bindings.

- DataConnection: DataConnection is a .NET class provided in the RuleEngine library. It contains a .NET SqlConnection instance and a DataSet name. The DataSet name enables you to create a unique identifier for the SqlConnection, and is used to define the resulting type. The DataConnection class provides a performance optimization to the Business Rule engine. Rather than asserting into the engine very large database tables (TypedDataTable class), which may contain many database rows (TypedDataRow class) that are not relevant to the policy, you could assert a lightweight DataConnection. When the engine evaluates a policy, it dynamically constructs a SELECT query based on the rule predicates/actions, and use it to query the DataConnection at execution.

- TypedDataTable: You can assert an ADO.NET DataTable object into the engine, but it will be treated like any other .NET object. TypedDataTable is a wrapper class that contains an ADO.NET DataTable. The constructor simply takes a DataTable. Any time a table or column in a table is used as a rule argument, the expression is evaluated against the individual TypedDataRow wrappers, and not against the TypedDataTable.

- TypedDataRow: This is a typed fact wrapper for an ADO DataRow object. Dragging a table or column to a rule argument in the Business Rule Composer results in rules built against the returned TypedDataRow wrappers.

160.   What is the difference between short-term and long-term facts?

A short-term fact is specific to a single execution cycle of the rule engine. Short-term facts are retracted automatically from the working memory of the rule engine after the policy executes. If your data changes between execution cycles of the rule engine for a policy, you submit the data as a short-term fact to the rule engine. A long-term fact is loaded into the working memory of the rule engine for use over an arbitrary number of execution cycles. Typically, long-term facts are slowly changing facts that do not change between executions of a policy.

161. What is the Business Rule Engine algorithm for policy execution?

The Business Rule Engine uses a three-stage algorithm for policy execution. These stages are:

- Match: Facts are matched against the predicates that use the fact type (object references maintained in the rule engine's working memory) using the predicates defined in the rule conditions. The output of the pattern-matching phase consists of updates to the rule engine agenda.

- Conflict resolution: Rules, which are candidates for execution, are examined to determine the next set of rule actions to execute based on a predetermined resolution scheme. All candidate rules found during the matching stage are added to the rule engine's agenda. The default conflict resolution scheme is based on rule priorities within a policy. The priority is a configurable property of a rule in the Business Rule Composer. The larger the number, the higher the priority; therefore if multiple rules are triggered, the higher-priority actions are executed first.

- Action: The actions in the resolved rule are executed. Note that rule actions can assert new facts into the rule engine, which causes the cycle to continue. This is also known as forward chaining. It is important to note that the algorithm never preempts the currently executing rule. All actions for the rule that is currently firing will be executed before the match phase is repeated. However, other rules on the agenda will not be fired before the match phase begins again. The match phase may cause those rules on the agenda to be removed from the agenda before they ever fire.

---

162. What are the BRE Control Functions?

The Business Rule Engine control functions are functions that allow an application or policy to control the facts in the rule engine's working memory. The presence of facts in the working memory drives the conditions that are evaluated, and the actions that are executed.

- Assert: Assertion is the process of adding object instances into the Business Rule engine's working memory. The engine processes each instance according to the conditions and actions that are written against the type of the instance, using the match-conflict resolution-action phases.

- Retract: The Retract function is used to remove objects from the Business Rule Engine's working memory.

- RetractByType: This function retracts all instances of a specified type in the working memory, whereas the Retract function retracts only specific items of a certain type.

- **Reassert**: To reassert means to call the Assert function on an object that is already in the engine's working memory. A reassert command is equivalent to issuing a retract command for the object, followed by an assert command.

- **Update**: You use the Update function to improve engine performance and prevent endless loop scenarios. In a typical scenario, an object is updated by a rule and then must be reasserted into the engine to be re-evaluated, based on the new data and state.

- **Halt**: The Halt function is used to stop the execution of the current rule engine. The Halt function takes one parameter of Boolean type. If you set the value of the parameter to true, the rule engine clears the agenda that contains the pending candidate rules.

163. What do you need to do to implement a custom Fact retriever?

You need to implement the IFactRetriever interface and configure a policy version to use this implementation at run time to bring in the long-term fact instances. The policy version invokes the UpdateFacts method of the fact retriever implementation on each execution cycle when a fact retriever is configured for that particular version. Optionally, you can also implement the IFactRemover interface on a fact retriever component. The rule engine invokes the UpdateFactsAfterExecution method of the IFactRemover interface when the policy is disposed. This provides an opportunity to you to do any post-execution work such as committing any database changes or retracting any object instances from the rule engine's working memory.

164. Does the rules engine support Transactions?

No. The rules engine does not support transactions in general. However, you can update a database in a transactional manner by using the DataConnection.

165. What is a rule priority?

Priority for execution is set on each individual rule, with a default priority of 0 for all rules. The priority can range on either side of the zero, with larger values meaning higher priority. Actions are executed in order from highest priority to lowest priority.

166. What is a Fact Creator?

A fact creator is a .Net object you use to create instances of your facts. Your fact creator must implement IFactCreator, a CreateFacts method, as well as a GetFactTypes method.

After you have created your fact creator DLL, you can browse to it from within the policy tester.

167. How to Test business rules?

To test a policy, you need facts on which the rules can be executed. You can add facts by specifying values in XML documents or database tables that you will point to in the policy tester, or you can use a fact creator to supply to the engine an array of .NET objects as facts. To test a policy in the Business Rule Composer:

1. In the Policy Explorer window, click the policy version that you want to test.

2. Click the Test Policy button (green arrow) on the menu bar.

3. The top pane displays the fact types that the policy rules reference.

4. To add a fact instance, click an XML Document or Database Table fact type, and then click Add Instance.

5. If you want to remove a fact instance, click the corresponding fact type, and then click Remove Instance.

6. If you want to add a fact creator that you have written, click Add in the fact creator pane.

7. Click Test.

8. The policy test trace output appears in the test output window.

168. How to deploy business rules into production?

Use the Rule Engine Deployment Wizard to deploy or undeploy a policy. Note that the Vocabularies must be deployed before polices.

169. How to Execute Business rules?

You can invoke a policy (or rule set) from an orchestration by using the Call Rules shape. The policy invokes the rule engine, which operates on the rules in the policy. Or you can use Microsoft.RuleEngine.Policy to invoke a policy from a .Net object.

BAM and BAS Questions

170. What is BAM?

Business Activity Monitoring (BAM) is a collection of tools that allow you to manage aggregations, alerts, and profiles to monitor relevant business metrics (called Key Performance Indicators – KPI's). These tools give you end-to-end visibility into your business processes, providing accurate information about the status and results of various operations, processes, and transactions, so that you can address problem areas and resolve issues within your business. The BAM Framework provides an easy, real-time, transaction-consistent way to monitor heterogeneous business applications, and to present data for SQL queries and aggregated reports (OLAP).

Through queries and aggregations you can include not only the data that is present during the running business process, but also the state and the dynamics of the running business process, which is independent of how the business is automated. BAM applies operational business intelligence and application integration technologies to automated processes to continually refine the automated processes based on feedback that comes directly from knowledge of operational events. In addition to auditing business processes (and business process management systems), BAM can send event-driven alerts that can be used to alert decision makers to changes in the business that may require action.

171. What is a BAM Activity?

A BAM activity represents a specific business process, such as handling purchase orders or shipping a product, and each one has a defined set of milestones and business data.

172. What is BAS?

Business Activity Services allows a business analyst to:

- Manage Trading Partners (Trading Partner Management): Creating business-to-business connections between trading partners. This component relies on a TPM database that stores information about trading relationships. Using the common Business Activity Services interface, information workers can create and modify agreements with trading partners who use BizTalk Server 2006. Each agreement describes the relationship between two parties, and the things it contains include:

- A profile for each of the partners. Each profile contains business information about the organization, such as a contact person and address, along with technical information such as the protocol (which determines the BizTalk Server adapter) that should be used to communicate with them.

- The business process itself, implemented as one or more orchestrations, along with the role each of the partners plays. One organization might act as the seller, for example, while the other acts as the buyer.

- An addendum with parameters for the business process that control the behavior of the orchestration implementing it. How these parameters are used is described in the next section.

- Configure Business Process: To enable information workers configure an orchestration, the developer creating it can define parameters for that orchestration. Information workers can then set these parameters as needed, for example, assigning different values for different business partners or different parts of their own organizations. An information worker sets those parameters using the TPM service, described in the previous section, by specifying their values in the addendum to this partner's agreement. For agreement that reference multiple orchestrations, an addendum can be created for each orchestration.

---

173. What is the BAM Add-in for Excel?

The BAM Add-In provides the tools you need to create a BAM observation model. A BAM observation model consists of three parts: a BAM activity, a BAM view, and a BAM aggregation. A BAM activity defines milestones and data of interest. A BAM view defines dimensions and measures based on the data of interest and milestones that present information to a particular audience. A BAM aggregation is a summary of the information defined in a view.

---

174. What is a BAM view?

A Business Activity Monitoring (BAM) view is the information from an activity which is intended for a particular audience. Views can contain both data and aggregations of data.

---

175. How to deploy a BAM definition file?

Open a Command Prompt window and execute the following command:

BM deploy-all -DefinitionFile:"difffilename.xls "

---

176.   What Is a BAM Activity?

A BAM activity is the definition of what data is interesting for an item in the business process (such as a single PO). It also defines the columns in the BAM database. An instance of an activity represents a unit of work in the business. An activity specifies a list of milestones (the history of the activity) and data of interest. An instance of an activity is manifested as a single row in the BAM Primary Import database. There is one and only one value for any data item for that instance of the activity.

177.   What Is a Continuation?

Continuations provide guidance to the BAM infrastructure about the following information:

- The order in which events are expected to occur, and
- A way to handle any change in the unique ID to which event items are correlated.

178.   What Is a Reference?

A reference (also known as a related activity) specifies a relationship between an activity and some other item.

Deployment and Installation

179. What are the best practices for deploying a BizTalk Application?

- Group related artifacts together in a single application: As much as possible, place related artifacts in the same BizTalk application.

- Deploy shared artifacts in a separate application: In situations where artifacts are going to be shared by two or more applications, deploy the shared artifacts into a separate application.

- Deploy a shared Web site in a separate application: In the case when a Web site will be shared by more than one business solution, deploy the Web site in a separate application.

- Deploy shared policies in a separate application: When a policy is used by two or more applications, you should deploy it in a separate application rather than creating a reference from one application to another.

- Deploy shared certificates in a separate application: When a certificate is used by a send port or receive location in two or more applications, you should deploy the certificate in a separate application, and then reference this application from the applications that need to use the certificate.

---

180. How to deploy a BizTalk solution from Development to Staging or to Production?

1. Export the BizTalk Application using the BizTalk Administration MMC.. Exporting a BizTalk application generates a Windows Installer (.msi) file that contains the application and any of its artifacts that you select to export.

2. Import the .msi file into staging or production BizTalk group to add the artifacts to an existing application in the new group.

3. Update the Bindings in the staging or production group.

4. If the application includes file-based artifacts, you must also install the artifacts it before the application can begin functioning.

181. How to deploy a BizTalk solution from Development to Staging or Production using the command line?

Use the following command line to export the BizTalk Application:

BTSTask ExportApp [/ApplicationName:value] /Package:value [ResourceSpec:value [/Server:value] [/Database:value]

Using the following command line to Import the BizTalk Application:

BTSTask ImportApp /Package: value [/Environment:value] [/ApplicationName:value] [/Overwrite] [/Server:value] [/Database:value]

---

182. What is the default application?

When BizTalk Server 2006 is configured following installation, a default application named BizTalk Application 1 is automatically created.

---

183. What is the BizTalk.System application?

When BizTalk Server 2006 is configured, following installation, an application named BizTalk.System is automatically created and populated with common artifacts which are used by all BizTalk applications, such as the default schemas and pipelines. BizTalk.System and its artifacts are read-only. You cannot delete or rename BizTalk.System, nor can you delete, rename, or move any of the artifacts that it contains.

---

184. How do you tune a BizTalk Solution?

You have to identify the different adapters, maps, orchestrations, pipelines and hosts used by the solution. You need to get performance results and determine the location of the bottle neck, if any. Based on that, you can modify the settings in the BTSNTSrvc.exe.Config, the IIS configurations setting, for tuning web services, IIS, and the ASP.NET worker process. For the CLR modify the machine.config. Persistence affects the overall system performance. Message parsing affects performance due to the incurred persistence points in the process. To tune the BizTalk solution and minimize the number of persistence points, change the Large Message Threshold and Fragment Size property of the BizTalk Server Group. The default value for this property is 1MB, meaning that each 1MB read from the message will result in a fragment being persisted to the MessageBox.

185. What are the known issues that might cause the MessageBox to be the performance bottleneck for a BizTalk Solution?

- The Biztalk Host instance that has the "allow Host tracking" option set is stopped. This is the host that is responsible for moving the tracking data from the MessageBox database to the Biztalk Tracking database(BizTalkDTADb).

- SQL Server Agent is not running: This can happen if the SQL jobs responsible for moving data from the MessageBox database to the BizTalkDTADb database [subsequently purging the moved data in the MessageBox] are not running.

- SQL Server Jobs are disabled Even if the SQL Server Agent is running, it is imperative that none of the default SQL Server jobs be disabled.

- BizTalkDTADb database grows excessively. This could happen when the BizTalkDTADb database grows very large, causing inserts into the BizTalkDTADb database to take longer. When this occurs, the movement of data by Tracking Data Delivery Service (TDDS) slows down, causing a backlog build up in the MessageBox database.

- Excessive Disk I/O Latency. If the incoming rate of data into the MessageBox database is faster than the rate at which the system can process and move the data to the BizTalkDTADb database, backlog could build up in the MessageBox database.

186. What is TCP/IP Port Exhaustion?

When a client initiates a TCP/IP socket connection to a server, the client typically connects to a specific port on the server and requests that the server responds to the client over an ephemeral, or short lived, TCP or UDP port. On Windows Server 2003, and Windows XP, the default range of ephemeral ports used by client applications is from 1,025 to 5,000. Under certain conditions it is possible that available ports in the default range be exhausted.

187. How can you scale a BizTalk Solution?

A BizTalk Server system has two tiers: the BizTalk Server tier and the SQL Server tier, which contains your MessageBox databases. In any scenario, you can scale out or scale up each tier. That is, you can scale-out BizTalk Server and the MessageBox database, or scale up both of them. You can have up to four BizTalk Servers in a group if you have the enterprise edition. Each server can have up to four processors. Depending on the issues with your environment, you might consider refactoring your solution host(s) so that you can have one server to do all the transmitting another one to do all the receiving, etc. If SQL Server is the issue then you might need to cluster and scale up your SQL servers.

188. How do you guarantee high availability of a BizTalk Solution?

You have to designing your BizTalk Server deployment to provide high availability. This involves implementing redundancy for each functional component involved in an application integration or business process integration scenario. So providing high availability for BizTalk Server 2006 involves running multiple host instances and clustering the BizTalk Server databases.

---

189. What are the BizTalk SQL Agent Jobs and what each one do?

- Backup BizTalk Server (BizTalkMgmtDb): It performs full database and log backups of the BizTalk Server databases.

- CleanupBTFExpiredEntriesJob_BizTalkMgmtDb: This cleans up expired BizTalk Framework (BTF) entries in the BizTalk Management (BizTalkMgmtDb) database.

- DTA Purge and Archive (BizTalkDTADb): It automatically archives data in the BizTalk Tracking (BizTalkDTADb) database and purges obsolete data.

- MessageBox_DeadProcesses_Cleanup_BizTalkMsgBoxDb: This job detects when a BizTalk Server host instance (NT service) has stopped and releases all work that was being done by that host instance so that it can be worked on by another host instance.

- MessageBox_Message_Cleanup_BizTalkMsgBoxDb: This removes all messages that are no longer being referenced by any subscribers in the BizTalk MessageBox (BizTalkMsgBoxDb) database tables.

- MessageBox_Message_ManageRefCountLog_BizTalkMsgBoxDb: This is used to manage the reference count logs for messages and determine when a message is no longer referenced by any subscriber.

- MessageBox_Parts_Cleanup_BizTalkMsgBoxDb: This removes all message parts that are no longer being referenced by any messages in the BizTalk MessageBox (BizTalkMsgBoxDb) database tables. All messages are made up of one or more message parts, which contain the actual message data.

- MessageBox_UpdateStats_BizTalkMsgBoxDb: This job manually updates the statistics for the BizTalk MessageBox (BizTalkMsgBoxDb) database.

- Operations_OperateOnInstances_OnMaster_BizTalkMsgBoxDb: This job is needed for multiple MessageBox deployments. It asynchronously performs operational actions such as bulk terminate on the master

MessageBox after those changes have been applied to the subordinate MessageBox.

- PurgeSubscriptionsJob_BizTalkMsgBoxDb: This job purges unused subscription predicates from the BizTalk Server MessageBox (BizTalkMsgBoxDb) database.

- Rules_Database_Cleanup_BizTalkRuleEngineDb: This job automatically purges old audit data from the Rule Engine (BizTalkRuleEngineDb) database every 90 days. This job also purges old history data (deploy/undeploy notifications) from the Rule Engine (BizTalkRuleEngineDb) database every 3 days.

- TrackedMessages_Copy_BizTalkMsgBoxDb: This job copies the messages bodies of tracked messages from the BizTalk Server MessageBox (BizTalkMsgBoxDb) database to the Tracking (BizTalkDTADb) database.

190. What is the Master Secret Server?

The master secret server is the Enterprise Single Sign-On (SSO) server that stores the master secret (encryption key). The master secret server generates the master secret when an SSO administrator requests it. The master secret server stores the encrypted master secret in the registry. Only Single Sign-On administrators can access the master secret. You cannot use the SSO system until an SSO administrator configures the master secret server and generates the master secret. The master secret server generates the master secret during configuration. Only SSO administrators can generate the master secret. An SSO administrator must configure the master secret server and the SSO database before an application can use the SSO service. If the master secret server fails, all runtime operations already running will continue to run, but SSO servers will not be able to encrypt new credentials.

191. What is the BTSTask?

BTSTask is a command-line tool that enables you to perform many administrative tasks from the command line, such as:

- Add a BizTalk application to the BizTalk Management database by using the AddApp command.

- Add an artifact to an application by using the AddResource command.

- Export an application and its artifacts to an .msi file by using the ExportApp command.

- Export binding information to an .xml file by using the ExportBindings command.

- Import an application from an .msi file by using the ImportApp command.

- Import binding information from an .xml file by using the ImportBindings command.

- List the artifacts included in an application along with their locally unique identifiers (LUIDs) by using the ListApp command.

- List all applications in the BizTalk Management database for the BizTalk group by using the ListApps command.

- List the resources in an .msi file by using the ListPackage command.

- List all of the artifact types supported by BizTalk Server 2006 by using the ListTypes command.

- Remove an application from the BizTalk Management database and the BizTalk Administration console by using the RemoveApp command.

- Remove an artifact from an application by using the RemoveResource command.

- Uninstall an application from the local computer by using the UninstallApp command.

192. What is Latency?

The time taken to process a message from receive end to send end.

193. What is Throttling?

Throttling is the mechanism by which the runtime engine prevents itself from thrashing and dropping dead when exposed to a high load. A properly throttled engine takes up only the amount of load that it can handle, and detects a stressed situation quickly and mitigates the situation accordingly.

194. How Many Database BizTalk needs?

BizTalk runtime operations require the use of four databases

1. BizTalk Management database(BizTalkMgmtDb): is the central meta-information store for all instances of BizTalk Server.

2. BizTalk MessageBox database(BizTalkMsgBoxDb): is used by the BizTalk Server engine for routing, queuing, instance management, and a variety of other tasks.

3. BizTalk Tracking database(BizTalkDTADb): stores health monitoring data tracked by the BizTalk Server tracking engine.

4. SSO database (SSODB): securely stores the configuration information for receive locations.

Depending on the BizTalk Server functionality that you use, you may have some or all of the following thirteen databases:

1. BAM Analysis (BAMAnalysis): contains Business Activity Monitoring (BAM) OLAP cubes for both online and offline analysis.

2. BAM Archive (BAMArchive): archives old business activity data. Create a BAM Archive database to minimize the accumulation of business activity data in the BAM Primary Import database.

3. BAM Notification Services Application database(BAMAlertsApplication) : contains alert information for BAM notifications. For example, when you create an alert using the BAM portal, entries are inserted in the database specifying the conditions and events to which the alert pertains, as well as other supporting data items for the alert.

4. BAM Notification Services Instance database(BAMAlertsNSMain): contains instance information specifying how the notification services connect to the system that BAM is monitoring.

5. BAM Primary Import database (BAMPrimaryImport): This is the database where BAM collects raw tracking data.

6. BAM Star Schema (BAMStarSchema): contains the staging table, and the measure and dimension tables.

7. BizTalk Base EDI database(BizTalkEDIdb): stores state for the Base electronic data interchange (EDI) adapter.

8. TPM database(TPM): stores trading partner data for Business Activity Services (BAS).

9. Tracking Analysis Server(BizTalkAnalysisDb): stores health monitoring online analytical processing (OLAP) cubes.

10. Windows SharePoint Services configuration database: contains all of the global settings for the server.

11. Windows SharePoint Services content database: contains all of the site content, such as list items and documents.

12. HWS Administration database(BizTalkHwsDb): contains all administration information related to Human Workflow Services (HWS).

13. Rule Engine database (BizTalkRuleEngineDb): is a repository for Policies, and Vocabularies.

195.   What is the BizTalk Application Users group?

This group includes all accounts with access to In-Process BizTalk hosts (hosts processes in BizTalk Server, BTSNTSvc.exe). It has BTS_HOST_USERS Server Database Role in the following databases:

- BizTalkMgmtDb
- BizTalkMsgBoxDb
- BizTalkRuleEngineDb
- BizTalkDTADb
- BAMPrimaryImport

And BAM_EVENT_WRITER SQL Server Database Role in the BAMPrimaryImport

196.   What are the BizTalk Services?

- BizTalk Base EDI Service: Processes EDI documents.
- BizTalk Service BizTalk Group: BizTalkServerApplication Provides the BizTalk Server application service.
- Enterprise Single Sign-On Service: Provides single sign-on services to enterprise applications.
- Rule Engine Update Service: Notifies users about the deployment or undeployment of policies.

197.   What are the BizTalk IIS Application Pools?

- BAMAppPool: Application pool for the BAM Portal.
- BTSSharePointAdapterWSAppPool: Application pool for the Windows SharePoint Service adapter Web service.
- HwsMessagesAppPool: Application pool for the HWS messaging component.
- HwsWSAppPool: Application pool for the HWS Web service.
- STSWebServiceAppPool: Application pool for the Trading Partner Management tools.
- TpmWSAppPool: Application pool for the TPM Management Web service

198. What are the tools and utilities you can use to troubleshoot a BizTalk Server?

- Event Viewer: When troubleshooting problems in a BizTalk Server component or dependency, the Event logs provides valuable information to help diagnose the problem.

- Network Monitor: Use the Network Monitor utility to capture network traffic between BizTalk Server and remote clients or servers. Captured network traffic can then be analyzed to diagnose network related problems.

- Fiddler Tool: Use Fiddler to record all HTTP traffic between BizTalk Server and remote clients or servers. Fiddlers allow you to save recordings as Web test files that can be added to Visual Studio Team Edition for Testers projects. An example of Fiddlers is available at http://www.fiddlertool.com.

- SQL Server Profiler: Microsoft SQL Server Profiler can be used to capture Transact-SQL statements that are sent to SQL Server and the SQL Server result sets from these statements. Since BizTalk Server is tightly integrated with SQL Server, the analysis of a SQL Server Profile trace can be a useful tool for analyzing problems that may occur in BizTalk Server when reading from and writing to SQL Server databases. For information about how to use SQL Server Profiler see the SQL Server documentation.

- SQL Server Query Analyzer and Query Editor: SQL Server Query Analyzer and SQL Server Query Editor can be used to execute SQL statements directly against SQL Server databases. This functionality may be useful for querying the BizTalk Server databases, or for updating the BizTalk Server databases in certain scenarios.

- DTCTester: Most BizTalk Server runtime operations require Microsoft Distributed Transaction Coordinator (MSDTC) support to ensure that the operations are transactionally consistent. If MSDTC transaction support is not available, then the associated BizTalk Server runtime operations cannot proceed. Use the DTCTester tool to verify distributed transaction support across firewalls or against networks. The DTCTester utility uses ODBC to verify transaction support against a SQL Server database and therefore requires that SQL Server is installed on one of the computers being tested.

- DTCPing: Use the DTCPing tool to verify distributed transaction support across firewalls or against networks. The DTCPing tool must be installed on both the client and server computer and is a good alternative to the DTCTester utility when SQL Server is not installed on either computer.

- Performance Console: Use the Performance Console to capture performance monitoring data in your BizTalk Server environment. See Performance Counters for a comprehensive list of the performance counters included with BizTalk Server.

- RegMon, FileMon, and DebugView:
    - o RegMon displays registry access activity in real time, listing each call to the registry that an application makes, and logging the outcome. This tool allows you to identify when an application cannot access a registry key. Similarly,
    - o FileMon displays file system activity in real time, listing each system call that an application makes and registering the outcome.
    - o Debugview lets you monitor debug output on your local system, or any computer on the network that you can reach via TCP/IP.

- Debug Diagnostics Tool of the IIS Diagnostics Toolkit: The Debug Diagnostic Tool of the IIS Diagnostics toolkit can generate a memory dump of a failing process and perform a basic analysis of the generated dump file.

199. How to Migrate BizTalk 2002 artifacts to BizTalk 2006?

The Migration Wizard migrates items from BizTalk Server 2002 to BizTalk Server 2006. The Migration Wizard uses Microsoft Windows integrated security to connect to the specified BizTalk MessageBox database. The Migration Wizard does not migrate scripting functoids used in BizTalk Server 2002 maps. They must be rewritten using one of the .NET Framework languages. The Migration Wizard converts BizTalk Server 2002 channels into receive pipelines and the corresponding ports into send pipelines. BizTalk Server 2006 uses a publish-and-subscribe (pub/sub) architecture making it unnecessary to have a send pipeline to publish the data into an orchestration. When the message arrives in the MessageBox database, BizTalk Server 2006 accesses the subscription, and invokes the orchestration which receives the message. You do not need to define a filter in your orchestration to receive a message, but you do need to configure the logical binding for the orchestration. The filter on the send ports may be more complex than you need, as it specifies filters on Organization and Application names that do not apply to BizTalk Server 2006. You may need to change or remove this filtering from the appropriate send ports.

200. How to Migrate BizTalk 2004 artifacts to BizTalk 2006?

When you perform an in-place upgrade from BizTalk Server 2004 to BizTalk Server 2006, all of your artifacts are automatically migrated and placed in the default application, BizTalk Application by default. This is because BizTalk Server 2004 did not include the concept of a BizTalk application, but all BizTalk Server 2006 artifacts must be associated with an application. You can then view and manage the artifacts from within the default application, or you can move them into separate applications in order to take advantage of the new application deployment features of BizTalk Server 2006.

Index

www.ingramcontent.com/pod-product-compliance
Lightning Source LLC
Chambersburg PA
CBHW060453060326
40689CB00020B/4512